Living in Ancient Egypt

EXPLORING
CULTURAL
HISTORY

Don Nardo, *Book Editor*

Daniel Leone, *President*
Bonnie Szumski, *Publisher*
Scott Barbour, *Managing Editor*

GREENHAVEN
PRESS ®

THOMSON
─ ─
GALE

San Diego • Detroit • New York • San Francisco • Cleveland
New Haven, Conn. • Waterville, Maine • London • Munich

© 2004 by Greenhaven Press. Greenhaven Press is an imprint of The Gale Group, Inc., a division of Thomson Learning, Inc.

Greenhaven® and Thomson Learning™ are trademarks used herein under license.

For more information, contact
Greenhaven Press
27500 Drake Rd.
Farmington Hills, MI 48331-3535
Or you can visit our Internet site at http://www.gale.com

Cover credit: © Archio Iconigrafico, S.A./CORBIS
Corel, 128
Dover Publications, 44
Library of Congress, 114

LIBRARY OF CONGRESS CATALOGING-IN-PUBLICATION DATA

Living in ancient Egypt / Don Nardo, book editor.
    p. cm. — (Exploring cultural history)
    Includes bibliographical references and index.
    ISBN 0-7377-1453-0 (pbk. : alk. paper) — ISBN 0-7377-1452-2 (lib. : alk. paper)
    1. Egypt—Social life and customs—To 332 B.C. I. Nardo, Don, 1947– . II. Series.
    DT61 .L785 2004
    932—dc21
                                                                    2002192518

Printed in the United States of America

Contents

Chapter 1: People and Private Life

Chapter 4: Secrets of the Royal Tombs

Foreword

Too often, history books and teachers place an overemphasis on events and dates. Students learn that key births, battles, revolutions, coronations, and assassinations occurred in certain years. But when many centuries separate these happenings from the modern world, they can seem distant, disconnected, even irrelevant.

The reality is that today's society is *not* disconnected from the societies that preceded it. In fact, modern culture is a sort of melting pot of various aspects of life in past cultures. Over the course of centuries and millennia, one culture passed on some of its traditions, in the form of customs, habits, ideas, and beliefs, to another, which modified and built on them to fit its own needs. That culture then passed on its own version of the traditions to later cultures, including today's. Pieces of everyday life in past cultures survive in our own lives, therefore. And it is often these morsels of tradition, these survivals of tried and true past experience, that people most cherish, take comfort in, and look to for guidance. As the great English scholar and archaeologist Sir Leonard Woolley put it, "We cannot divorce ourselves from our past. We are always conscious of precedents . . . and we let experience shape our views and actions."

Thus, for example, Americans and the inhabitants of a number of other modern nations can pride themselves on living by the rule of law, educating their children in formal schools, expressing themselves in literature and art, and following the moral precepts of various religions and philosophies. Yet modern society did not invent the laws, schools, literature, art, religions, and philosophies that pervade it; rather, it inherited these things from previous cultures. "Time, the great destroyer, is also the great preserver," the late, noted thinker Herbert J. Muller once observed. "It has preserved . . . the immense accumulation of products, skills, styles, customs, institutions, and ideas that make the man on the American street indebted to all the peoples of history, including some who never saw a street." In this way, ancient Mesopotamia gave the world its first cities and literature; ancient Egypt, large-scale architecture; ancient Israel, the formative concepts of Judaism,

Christianity, and Islam; ancient Greece, democracy, the theater, Olympic sports, and magnificent ceramics; ancient China, gunpowder and exotic fabrics; ancient Rome and medieval England, their pioneering legal systems; Renaissance Italy, great painting and sculpture; Elizabethan England, the birth of modern drama; and colonial America, the formative environments of the founders of the United States, the most powerful and prosperous nation in world history. Only by looking back on those peoples and how they lived can modern society understand its roots.

Not all the products of cultural history have been so constructive, however. Most ancient Greeks severely restricted the civil rights and daily lives of women, for instance; the Romans kept and abused large numbers of slaves, as did many Americans in the years preceding the Civil War; and Nazi Germany and the Soviet Union curbed or suppressed freedom of speech, assembly, and religion. Examining these negative aspects of life in various past cultures helps to expose the origins of many of the social problems that exist today; it also reminds us of the ever-present potential for people to make mistakes and pursue misguided or destructive social and economic policies.

The books in the Greenhaven Press Exploring Cultural History series provide readers with the major highlights of life in human cultures from ancient times to the present. The family, home life, food and drink, women's duties and rights, childhood and education, arts and leisure, literacy and literature, roads and means of communications, slavery, religious beliefs, and more are examined in essays grouped by theme. The essays in each volume have been chosen for their readability and edited to manageable lengths. Many are primary sources. These original voices from a past culture echo through the corridors of time and give the volume a strong feeling of immediacy and authenticity. The other essays are by historians and other modern scholars who specialize in the culture in question. An annotated table of contents, chronology, and extensive bibliography broken down by theme add clarity and context. Thus, each volume in the Greenhaven Press Exploring Cultural History series opens a unique window through which readers can gaze into a distant time and place and eavesdrop on life in a long vanished culture.

Introduction: The Ancient Egyptians at Work and at Play

A s late as 1930, many (though certainly not all) modern scholars still perpetuated an image of the ancient Egyptians that has since been shown to be misguided. Namely, Egyptians of all social classes were pictured as so mired in tradition, formal religion, and preparation for death and the afterlife that they were a somber, serious, stiff, and joyless people. In this view, moreover, the common peasants lived only to perform the whims of the nobles and priests and were therefore downtrodden, bereft of hope, and particularly cheerless. One of the leading classical scholars of the early twentieth century wrote in a highly acclaimed and widely read book:

> In Egypt the center of interest was in the dead. . . . Countless numbers of human beings for countless numbers of centuries thought of death as that which was nearest and most familiar to them. . . . To the Egyptian, the enduring world of reality was not the one he walked in . . . but the one he should presently go to by way of death. . . . [One cause for this] was human misery. The state of the common man . . . must have been wretched in the extreme. . . . Nothing so cheap as a human life in Egypt. . . . [So] Egypt submitted and suffered and turned her face toward death. . . . Wretched people, toiling people, do not play. Nothing like the Greek games is conceivable in Egypt. . . . If fun and sport had played any real part [in the Egyptians' lives] they would be in [the archaeological record] in some form for us to see. But the Egyptians did not play.[1]

This assessment of the ancient Egyptian outlook on life turned out to be mistaken. It is true that most Egyptians worked long hours, enjoyed few luxuries, had short life expectancies, and placed an emphasis on preparation for death and the afterlife. Yet, as scholar James F. Romano points out:

> In surveying the evidence that survives from antiquity, we are left with the overall impression that most Egyptians loved life and were willing to overlook its hardships. Indeed, the perfect afterlife was merely an ideal version of their earthly existence. Only the travails [toils] and petty annoyances that bothered them in

their lifetimes would be missing [in the afterlife]; all else, they hoped, would be as it was on earth.[2]

Indeed, abundant evidence is now available that the Egyptians, both wealthy and poor, both nobles and peasants, enjoyed and participated in numerous sports and games. Just as people in modern societies do, they integrated play with work the best way they could and found a satisfying balance between the two. This balance can be better understood by examining the Egyptians both at work and at play.

The Privileged vs. the Working Classes

Before considering working Egyptians, it must be pointed out that a few privileged and fortunate individuals in Egypt did no work at all. These included the pharaohs, the so-called god-kings who ruled the country, as well as other members of that country's upper classes. They enjoyed an existence largely free from want. They had power and prestige, servants to do the menial work, plenty of free time to pursue leisure pursuits, fine clothes, and numerous luxuries in their homes. It is not surprising that so much is known about how these nobles lived. As in other historical ages, most contemporary writers dwelled on the nobles and their lives. Also, a majority of the surviving archaeological evidence, including statues, furniture, weapons, inscriptions, paintings, and so forth, relates to the members of the upper classes.

However, the vast majority of ancient Egyptians—those making up the country's workforce—were ordinary folk. They were farmers, construction laborers, and craftsmen—whose names and deeds were rarely if ever recorded and quickly forgotten. For the most part, the evidence for how they lived comes from two sources. First are the accounts of Greek and Roman writers who visited or lived in Egypt during the late first millennium B.C. and early first millennium A.D. (In that era the country, no longer an independent nation, was ruled by Greeks and Romans.) Supplementing these accounts are discoveries made by archaeologists. Their efforts continue, and each year excavations reveal new papyri (documents written on papyrus, a parchment made from a water plant), houses, gravesites, tools, pottery, figurines, personal items, and other artifacts shedding light on the everyday life of common people.

Though the lives of these commoners did revolve primarily around work, their existence was not, in the larger scheme of things, simply a matter of year-to-year labor and bare subsistence with nothing to show for it in the long run. Inspired and/or guided by the nobles, over the course of many generations the Egyptian people created one of the world's first, greatest, and most enduring civilizations. Their accomplishment is all the more remarkable considering that they inhabited a land of significant physical extremes. Then, as now, Egypt was made up mainly of dry desert wastelands; and nearly all of the people dwelled in a narrow, highly fertile strip of land bordering the Nile River,

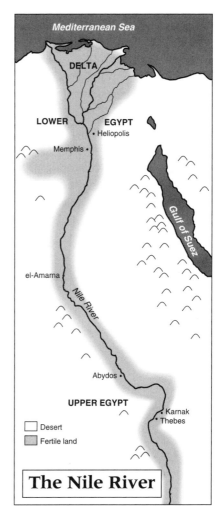

The Nile River

which flows from the highlands of Ethiopia in the south to the Mediterranean Sea in the north.

Within that long green ribbon of fertile land, the commoners built their homes, worked, played, worshiped, and died. For thousands of years, they were almost completely dependent on the Nile River, which supplied the water they needed for drinking, cooking, bathing, washing clothes, and irrigating crops. The Egyptians also used the river to mark the passage of time and the seasons. From June to September or October, for example, the Nile flooded, covering the nearby fields with water and depositing a fresh layer of rich soil.

Farmers and Their Crops

This soil was absolutely crucial to Egyptian life, especially to the farmers, mostly peasants who made up the bulk of the country's population and workforce. As Egyptologist Fekri Hassan explains:

> The civilization of Egypt and its spectacular achievements were based throughout its history on the prosperity of a mainly agrarian [farming] economy. The country's verdant green fields and bountiful food resources depended on the fertile soil of the Nile flood-plain and the annual summer flood. . . . As soon as the waters began to recede, the farmers returned to their sodden fields to sow their seeds. The crops were ready for harvest from February to early June, when the Nile was at its lowest level.[3]

These crops included emmer wheat and barley, from which the people made bread and beer; peas, lentils, cucumbers, leeks, onions, radishes, and other vegetables; dates, melons, figs, grapes, and other fruits; herbs to make medicines; flax for making fibers for clothes; and papyrus.

The planters often sang work songs, one of which went:

> A good day—it is cool.
> The cattle are pulling,
> And the sky does according to our desire.
> Let us work for the noble![4]

(The phrase "Let us work for the noble" was a reference to the fact that peasant farmers usually did not own the land on which they worked. Most arable land in ancient Egypt belonged to the pharaoh, his nobles, or the religious temples; they collected the bulk of the crops, and the farmers kept a modest portion for themselves and their families.)

Although growing and harvesting crops was a farmer's principal activity, many other chores and duties, most of them mundane and repetitious, kept him busy. A surviving document used in the schools attended by the country's tiny elite educated class describes some of the tougher aspects of a farmer's life (in a disparaging tone since members of the upper classes looked on the peasants as socially inferior):

> During the inundation [Nile flood] he [the farmer] is wet through, but he must attend to his equipment all the same. He passes the whole day making and repairing his farming tools, and the whole

night twisting rope. Even his midday lunch hour he spends doing farming work. . . . At dawn he goes out to look after the team [of oxen he was using to clear tree stumps and rocks from his plot] and does not find it where he left it. He spends three days searching for the oxen and finds them stuck in the bog, dead; and there are no hides on them either; the jackals have chewed them up.[5]

After a hard day's work, the farmers returned to their houses, which stood near the fields or in small rural villages located nearby. An average agricultural peasant's house featured walls made of mud bricks. The ceiling was fashioned from bundles of plant stems, and the floors consisted of hard-beaten earth covered by a layer of straw or mats made from reeds. There were one or two rooms (perhaps occasionally three) in which the farmer and his wife and children (if any) lived. In many cases, they stabled some or all of their farm animals in the same rooms. Because such modest homes lacked bathrooms, the residents had to use an outside latrine (a hole in the ground) to relieve themselves. Needless to say, water had to be hauled in buckets from the river or the nearest hand-dug well.

Some of the water the peasant farmer and his family brought into the house was used for cooking. This was done on the hearth, which was most often a single flat slab of stone. Because the average peasant could not afford wood or charcoal, the fuel consisted of dried reeds, straw, or animal droppings. The farmer's wife cooked the food in earthenware pots.

The Pyramid Workers

Because it was not possible to farm the land during the yearly inundation, most farmers did have at least some free time during those months. A few took the time to rest. And perhaps some others turned to making pottery and other handicrafts. However, a good many of these idle farmers labored on government-sponsored projects, including the building of pyramids, temples, and other large stone structures. Thus, the Egyptian laborers who erected the pyramids were not slaves, as so often depicted in Hollywood films.

Most of the pyramid workers lived in large camps set up near the construction sites. These villagelike camps included not only areas for storing and preparing the stone and other building materials but also small houses with sleeping quarters for the workers and their families. Prominent as well were facilities for food production, including well-equipped bakeries. Describing some bakeries found at a large camp excavated south of the great pyramids at Giza, Egyptian archaeologist Zahi Hawass writes:

> Each bakery was about 17 feet long and eight feet wide. Inside each room lay a pile of broken bread pots discarded after the last batch of bread was removed 4,600 years ago. Though Egyptian written records attest at least 14 types of bread, we found only small and large bell-shaped pots and flat trays. Along the east wall were two lines of holes in a shallow trench, resembling an egg carton. The holes had held dough-filled pots while hot coals and ash in the trench baked the bread. A hearth in the southeastern corner would have been used to heat pots before they were inverted as lids on dough-filled containers in the trench.[6]

The workers' camp also contained a cemetery with tombs for those laborers who died while on the job. These were much smaller and more humble than the monumental royal pyramid tombs that towered above them. But as modern excavators discovered, these gravesites reveal much about the lives and customs of the everyday Egyptians who were interred in them, including such details as their names, marital status, hairstyles, and general life expectancy. According to Hawass:

> The lower part of the cemetery contains about 600 such graves for workmen and 30 larger tombs, perhaps for overseers. The tombs come in a variety of forms: stepped domes, beehives, and gabled roofs. Two to six feet high, the domes covered simple rectangular grave pits, following the configuration of the pyramids in an extremely simplified form. One small tomb featured a miniature ramp leading up and around its dome. Could the builder have intended it to represent the construction ramp of a royal pyramid?. . . We have found many false doors and stelae [marker stones] attached to these tombs. . . . Inscribed in crude hieroglyphs, they record the names of the people whose skeletons lay below. . . . Small stone figurines in a rectangular niche. . . . represent [the members of] a household of these workers. One of the statuettes depicts a woman seated on a backless chair with her hands on her knees. . . . She wears a black wig with hair parted in the middle and reaching to her shoulders. . . . Study of the [skeletal] remains [of those buried in the cemetery] . . . reveals that males and females were equally represented, mostly

buried in fetal positions, with face to the east and head to the north. Many of the men died between the age of 30 and 35. Below the age of 30, a higher mortality was found in females . . . undoubtedly reflecting the hazards of childbirth.[7]

The tombs and burial rituals of the pyramid workers and other lower-class Egyptians reveal how important religion was in their lives. Like the pharaohs, nobles, and priests, the vast majority of working-class Egyptians devoutly worshiped a large group of gods and believed in an afterlife. Every person hoped that after death his or her soul would travel into the underworld, ruled by the god Osiris, where life was comfortable, carefree, and eternal. So even the modest graves of the construction laborers contained offerings of food, toiletries, tools, weapons, and other material objects that the deceased might need during his or her journey to the realm of the dead.

Craftsmen and Miners

Members of the Egyptian working classes also included craftsmen, who possessed special skills that were always in high demand. They created pottery vases, bowls, pitchers, plates, and drinking cups; wooden chairs, tables, storage chests, and other furniture items; wall paintings, sculpted bas-reliefs for the palaces and noble houses, and statues of all sizes; and exquisite jewelry and other objects made from gems and both precious and non-precious metals. Many of the artifacts turned out by these artisans have been found by modern excavators beneath the remains of palaces, temples, townhouses, and, on occasion, inside tombs. (Unfortunately, the contents of most wealthy burial sites were long ago plundered by grave robbers.)

The best-preserved and most famous example of an Egyptian tomb containing objects made by the artisan class is that of the relatively obscure pharaoh Tutankhamen, or "King Tut," discovered during the 1920s. The tomb contained more than two thousand beautifully crafted objects. Only a partial list includes chariots, boats, decorated chests, statues, jewelry, perfume boxes, a throne inlaid with gold and jewels, weapons with intricately carved handles, and a gaming board with ivory pieces.

Today, craftsmen with the skills to produce such artifacts are seen as professional artists, highly respected in society and extremely well paid. "But in the ancient Egyptian view," noted scholar Lionel Casson writes, "they were just craftsmen, to be paid in rations like all other workmen." Similarly, on the work-site artisans were treated like other laborers, benefiting from the same advantages and suffering from the same disadvantages. "In good times," says Casson,

> working conditions were not at all bad. The men did a ten-day shift, after which they got a certain amount of time off. And the authorities seem to have been lenient about absence; it was allowed not only for sickness, but for nursing the sick. Sickness itself was liberally interpreted. One man was excused from work because—or so he alleged—he had been beaten up by his wife. But when times were bad the men suffered. Their wages were not paid, and this meant that they simply went hungry.[8]

The worst working conditions for Egyptian laborers by far were in the mines, which supplied the gold, silver, and copper the craftsmen used to make hundreds of different products. In fact, in contrast with what the artisans themselves endured, Egyptian miners toiled under horrendous conditions. A Greek geographer, Agatharchides, described such workers and their plight in a gold mine during the second century B.C., when Egypt was under Greek rule. At the time, most of the workers were convicts and prisoners of war, in many cases accompanied by their wives, children, and other relatives, who had been imprisoned along with them. But conditions were likely not much different for the free laborers who toiled in Egypt's mines earlier, under the pharaohs of the Old, Middle, and New kingdoms. According to Agatharchides:

> The rock of the mountains in which the gold is found is sheer and very hard. They burn wood fires and render it spongy with heat, and then go at working it, cutting the parts softened up with quarrying tools. . . . Those who are young and strong quarry the gleaming stone with iron picks, delivering their blows not with any particular skill but just force. . . . They do their quarrying with [small oil] lamps bound to their foreheads, following the white gleam like a vein. Constantly shifting the position of their bodies, they knock down chunks—not according to their bodily condition and strength, but to the foreman's eye, who never fails to administer punishment with the whip. Young boys, creeping through the galleries hacked out by the miners, laboriously col-

lect what has fallen down on the gallery floor and carry it outside the entrance. From them the rock is taken over by the more elderly and many of the feeble, who bring it to the so-called choppers. . . . They pound the rock vigorously with iron pestles until they have made the biggest piece the size of a pea. . . . Now starts the work of the women who were arrested and put in custody along with their husbands or parents. A large number of grinding mills are placed in a row, and the pounded rock is put in them. The women take their places, three to a turning bar, and grind away. They are a sad sight, their clothes girded up and just enough to cover their private parts. . . . All who suffer the fate just described feel that death is more desirable than life.[9]

The sufferings of the gold miners clearly show that there was a heavy price paid by some people in society for the finer things enjoyed by some others.

Ball Games and Water Sports

Yet no matter how difficult, menial, or monotonous the tasks of Egyptian workers might be, their lives did not consist only of ceaseless toil. Like people in other places and ages, they enjoyed recreation and leisure activities when time and circumstances permitted. Mostly they played fairly simple games, including various ones involving balls. A surviving wall painting shows two girls throwing a small ball back and forth while several of their friends keep time for them by clapping their hands. Another painting shows a group of children playing in pairs; in each pair one child carries the other piggyback while the children on top toss a ball to one another.

Perhaps because the mighty Nile was so close at hand, working-class Egyptians also enjoyed water sports and games, apparently the more vigorous the better. A common one played by boys and men was "water jousting," which featured a contest between two canoes (small, simple boats fashioned from bundled plant stems). The crew of each canoe included one or more oarsmen and one "fighter," who stood upright and brandished a long stick. As the oarsmen maneuvered the boats, jockeying for advantage, the fighters attempted to knock each other into the water.

An even more exciting and decidedly more dangerous water sport consisted of "shooting" (riding through) the Nile's rapids. At various locations the river has cataracts, places where the ground level changes height, causing the water to flow into rapids of varying states of turbulence. The first-century A.D. Roman playwright Seneca the Younger, who owned land in Egypt, called a cataract "a remarkable spectacle." There, he said, the water

> surges through rocks which are steep and jagged in many places, and unleashes its forces . . . in a violent torrent [that] leaps forward through narrow passages. . . . Finally, it struggles through the obstructions in its way, and then, suddenly losing its support, falls down an enormous depth with a tremendous crash that echoes through the surrounding regions.[10]

Seneca watched in awe and delight as native Egyptians challenged these torrents in death-defying displays:

> The people . . . embark on small boats, two to a boat, and one rows while the other bails out water. Then they are violently tossed about in the raging rapids. . . . At length they reach the narrowest channels . . . and, swept along by the whole force of the river, they control the rushing boat by hand and plunge head downward to the great terror of the onlookers. You would believe sorrowfully that by now they were drowned and overwhelmed by such a mass of water, when far from the place where they fell, they shoot out as from a catapult, still sailing, and the subsiding wave does not submerge them, but carries them on to smooth waters.[11]

"I'll Make You Cringe with Fear"

In particular, working-class Egyptians (along with members of the upper classes) looked forward to a few major religious festivals held each year. During these celebrations, they took part in various informal leisure activities, among them dancing, running, tug-of-war contests, and especially wrestling. In fact, wrestling may have been the most popular and widely played of all sports pursued in ancient Egypt.

Incredibly, if he had a time machine that allowed him to travel to the present day, a skilled Egyptian wrestler would immediately be able to adapt to modern wrestling styles, both amateur and professional. A series of about four hundred wall paintings dating from the Middle Kingdom and unearthed at Beni Hasan, on the Nile in central Egypt, shows wrestlers applying many of the same moves and holds used in today's amateur and professional ranks. Classic armlocks, headlocks, and bodylocks are common in the paintings. Also depicted are trips, shoulder throws, flying mares, and many others.

More ominous are illustrations of wrestlers choking each other. Whether choking was a legal tactic in Egypt remains unclear. However, evidence indicating that it was probably foul play was found in a later Egyptian sculpture showing a wrestling exhibition before one of the pharaohs. Next to a scene of a grappler applying a choke hold is an inscription that reads, "Take care! You are in the presence of the Pharaoh!"[12]

These paintings and sculptures show that Egyptian wrestling featured other aspects common to the game today. For instance, the matches were mediated by referees. Also, wrestlers used the "psyche-out" technique, in which one fighter tries to instill fear in the other through boasts and taunts (a tactic raised to a humorous art by modern professional wrestlers). In the Beni Hasan murals, an inscription quotes one wrestler telling his opponent, "I'm going to pin you! I'll make you weep in your heart and cringe with fear. Look, I'm going to make you fall and faint away right in front of the Pharaoh!"[13]

Royal Hunters and Rowers

Speaking of the pharaoh, he, too, along with his nobles, took part in various sports and games. High on the list of leisure pursuits enjoyed by Egypt's rich and famous set was hunting, and a number of accounts of royal hunts have survived. In one, a scribe of the pharaoh Amenhotep III (reigned 1390–1352 B.C.) boasts that "the total number of lions killed by His Majesty with his own arrows, from the first to the tenth year [of his reign] was 102 wild lions."[14] Another pharaoh, Thutmosis III (reigned 1479–1425 B.C.) claimed that he dispatched 120 elephants, bragging in an inscription, "No king has ever done such a thing since the world began!"[15]

It must be emphasized that such accounts shaded the truth in an attempt to make the monarchs look more accomplished than they really were. The pharaohs did not generally hunt dangerous creatures such as lions and elephants in the wild. Instead, royal game wardens first captured the animals and put them in special fenced-in areas, where, closely guarded by armed soldiers, a pharaoh stalked and killed his prey. When hunting less dangerous animals, such as antelope, wild cattle, and donkeys, a ruler might actually venture out into the desert.

As for the methods used for such hunts, the pharaoh or other noble typically used a chariot. An expert driver operated the vehicle, which allowed the upper-class hunter to wield his weapons—either a bow and arrow or a lance—with both hands. This style of hunting gave rise to another popular sport—shooting at fixed targets from moving chariots. Some pharaohs actually displayed their shooting talents in public performances. A surviving sculptured relief shows the pharaoh Amenhotep II (reigned 1427–1400 B.C.) firing his bow from a moving chariot, with an inscription below reading, "His Majesty performed these feats before the eyes of the whole land."[16] (Actually, attendance at such displays was probably restricted to members of the upper classes and selected army units.)

Amenhotep II also enjoyed one of the favorite pastimes of the ancient Egyptian nobility—rowing, as shown in another of his inscriptions. "His arms were so strong," the text reads,

> that he was never faint when he grasped the oar and rowed his arrow-swift ship, the best of the crew of two-hundred. Many were faint after a course of half a mile, exhausted and weary of limb and out of shape; but His Majesty still rowed powerfully.[17]

Once again, it is likely that the scribe who carved the inscription shaded the truth to bolster the king's image. It was customary in Egyptian art to depict the ruler as both physically and mentally superior to his subjects. Nevertheless, this account, along with many others, gives a clear picture of the Egyptian nobility at play.

Images of nobles and common folk variously hunting, boating, fishing, wrestling, dancing, playing ball, and frolicking in the water obviously belie the frequent and inaccurate portrayal of the ancient Egyptians as a cheerless, downtrodden population. As James Romano reminds us, they were in reality "a fun-loving people who filled their leisure hours with pleasant diversions." If one examines more recent evidence, he says, there emerges "a reasonably accurate picture of" their daily lives, in which work and play are skillfully balanced. "Their lives were certainly ordered," Romano adds, "but we never sense that they felt constrained by their rules and traditions. The Egyptians loved life and hoped to perpetuate its most pleasant aspects in the hereafter."[18]

Notes

1. Edith Hamilton, *The Greek Way to Western Civilization.* New York: New American Library, 1930, pp. 13, 18–19.

2. James F. Romano, *Daily Life of the Ancient Egyptians.* Pittsburgh: Carnegie Museum of Natural History, 1990, p. 49.

3. Quoted in David P. Silverman, ed., *Ancient Egypt.* New York: Oxford University Press, 1997, pp. 11–12.

4. Quoted in James B. Pritchard, ed., *Ancient Near Eastern Texts Relating to the Old Testament.* Princeton, NJ: Princeton University Press, 1969, p. 469.

5. Quoted in Sergio Donadoni, ed., *The Egyptians,* trans. Robert Bianchi et al. Chicago: University of Chicago Press, 1990, p. 17.

6. Zahi Hawass and Mark Lehner, "Builders of the Pyramids," *Archaeology,* January/February 1997, p. 34.

7. Zahi Hawass, "Tombs of the Pyramid Builders," *Archaeology,* January/February 1997, pp. 39–43.

8. Lionel Casson, *Daily Life in Ancient Egypt.* New York: American Heritage, 1975, pp. 75–76.

9. Quoted in Casson, *Daily Life in Ancient Egypt,* p. 77.

10. Seneca, *Seneca: Dialogues and Letters,* trans. and ed. in C.D.N. Costa. New York: Penguin Books, 1997, p. 110.

11. Seneca, *Natural Questions,* pp. 110–11.

12. Quoted in Michael B. Poliakoff, *Combat Sports in the Ancient World.* New Haven, CT: Yale University Press, 1987, p. 27.

13. Quoted in Gerald W. Morton and George M. O'Brien, *Wrestling to Rasslin: Ancient Sport to American Spectacle.* Bowling Green, OH: Bowling Green State University Press, 1985, p. 7.

14. Quoted in Vera Olivova, *Sports and Games in the Ancient World.* New York: St. Martin's, 1984, p. 49.

15. Quoted in Casson, *Daily Life in Ancient Egypt,* p. 49.

16. Quoted in Olivova, *Sports and Games,* p. 51.

17. Quoted in Olivova, *Sports and Games,* p. 51.

18. Romano, *Daily Life of the Ancient Egyptians,* pp. 38, 2.

People and Private Life

CHAPTER

1

Chapter Preface

About the year 2450 B.C., an Egyptian sage wrote: "If you are a man of standing, you should found your household and love your wife at home, as is fitting. Fill her belly; clothe her back. Ointment is the prescription for her body [i.e., make sure to buy her perfume]. Make her heart glad as long as you live. She is a profitable field for her lord [husband]." With these words the sage summed up most of the basic precepts of private life in ancient Egypt. First, the primary duty of a man was to establish a household and marry a woman. Moreover, he was expected to provide for her as best as he could, furnishing her with whatever foods, clothes, and personal gifts that he could afford to make her happy. She would then, presumably, reciprocate by keeping the household and bearing and rearing children to the best of her own ability.

That the sage's statement, along with other surviving Egyptian writings, emphasizes men's responsibilities toward women, as well as the concept of a woman's happiness, is revealing. In most ancient societies, women were little more than property in the eyes of most men; and the emphasis in those societies was almost always on how *women* could or should make *men* happy. Granted, like other ancient lands, Egypt was largely male-dominated and for the most part women were expected to do their husbands' bidding. Still, many Egyptian couples seem to have enjoyed positive, loving relationships. Part of the evidence consists of a number of love songs that have survived from ancient Egypt. In addition, upper-class husbands and wives dined, held parties, and went hunting together, while both well-to-do and poorer women shared many legal rights with men. In fact, ancient Egyptian women seem to have enjoyed more freedom in their private lives than women in most other ancient societies, even if men made most of the really important decisions.

Egyptian men benefited from positive, loving relationships as much as their wives did. Even if he was not deeply in love with his wife, a man could find a measure of happiness in the knowledge that she was content, willingly kept a tidy, well-managed home, and taught the children good manners. He could also take pride in the fact that he worked hard to put food on the table and a roof over both their heads.

This does not mean that the only joy in private life derived from household relationships and duties. Though leisure hours were few for the working classes, ordinary people filled these hours with sports and games whenever possible. (The wealthy could afford to engage in such activities much more often, of course.) Far from being a somber, downtrodden people who seldom played—an image often depicted in early modern writings—the Egyptians swam, hunted, rowed, played ball, wrestled, danced, played tug-of-war, and tinkered with board games.

Engaging in or watching such leisure activities was the only form of entertainment available in a society without radio, television, movies, and shopping malls. Along with marital respect and love and a well-managed house, playing games helped to keep both husband and wife content; and as the sage concluded, a household that knew happiness would long thrive.

Family and Home Life

Charles Freeman

As explained here by popular historian Charles Freeman, the family unit was integral to Egyptian society. Freeman summarizes the positions of women and children in a male-dominated social structure and also describes the houses of both common and well-to-do citizens. Freeman documents his presentation by citing archaeological evidence, in particular that from Deir el-Medina, on the Nile's west bank near the Valley of the Kings, where archaeologists have unearthed the unusually well-preserved remains of a town occupied by everyday Egyptian workers.

The family was the living unit of Egyptian society. Wall paintings and sculptures show contented couples with their arms around each other, and there was an ideal of care of young for old. 'Repay your mother for all her care to you,' writes one scribe. 'Give her as much bread as she needs and carry her as she has carried you. . . . For three years she suckled you, nor did she shrink from your dirt.' The evidence from Deir el-Medina suggests, however, that things did not always run smoothly in family life. Infidelity and jealousy were as common in ancient Egypt as elsewhere.

Women's Roles

Marriage took place for women at the onset of puberty, between 12 and 14, while men seem to have been older, perhaps 20, with those in the administrative élite having already begun to earn a living by then. It seems that both families had to provide goods before a marriage contract could be made, another incentive for gathering wealth. Within the royal family it was possible for a brother to marry a sister. (The legend of Isis and Osiris legitimized, or was developed to legitimize, the practice.) For commoners brother-sister marriages were almost unheard-of, although marriages between cousins and uncles and nieces were quite common.

Charles Freeman, *Egypt, Greece, and Rome: Civilizations of the Ancient Mediterranean.* New York: Oxford University Press, 1996. Copyright © 1996 by Charles Freeman. Reproduced by permission of the publisher.

Women normally followed what would now be seen as a highly traditional pattern of life, running the household and being expected to produce a male heir to carry on the family and to take responsibility for the family tomb. It was wives who, either personally or through servants, ground corn, baked bread, spun flax, and wove cloth from it. The job was not without its status and there was some acceptance of women's rights. Men were specifically warned to leave the running of the house to their wives, and women did have the right to own and manage property and could bring a case in court if they were dispossessed of it. A woman who was divorced by her husband became entitled to his continued support. . . . There may have been some emotional equality between the sexes.

In wall paintings women are usually portrayed as much lighter-skinned than their husbands. This may partly be convention but also presumably reflects the longer hours they spent within the home. (Light skin, a sign that a woman did not have to work in the sun, suggested high status.) Women are shown helping their husbands in the fields, and an inscription from the late New Kingdom suggests they could travel around freely outside the home. However, there are very few examples of women earning a living independently. There were some openings in the temples as junior priestesses or leaders of choruses but a more likely role was as an entertainer at feasts or as a member of the royal harem. (The kings had elaborate harems and one portrayal of Ramses III shows him relaxing in one.) . . .

Children

It was not expensive to keep children. They could run around naked in the warm air and live on papyrus roots. However, the mortality rate was high, especially at the moment of weaning. When boys reached the age of 14 they passed into adult life after a religious ceremony which included circumcision. On one occasion, in the First Intermediate Period, 120 boys are recorded as being circumcised at the same time, an indication that this was an important *rite de passage* recognized by the whole community. Girls stayed at home, and seem to have had no equivalent ceremony other than that of marriage.

By the age of 14 boys would already have received some training in their father's occupation, either through learning on the job or through formal instruction in a temple school. (Some records suggest formal education may have begun as early as 5.) For future administrators the course was a demanding one and total commitment was expected. 'I am told you neglect your studies and think only of pleasure. You wander through the streets, stinking of beer and have been found performing acrobatics on a wall', was the poor report given by a scribe to one of his students. It may have taken twelve years to master all the skills required to be a scribe. (The skills demanded went far beyond learning to write. A scribe would be expected to master all the details of administration, what rations a soldier should be given, how many bricks were needed to build a ramp, and how many men to pull and erect a stone statue, for instance.)

Houses

Another important use of wealth was the construction of a home. The houses of Deir el-Medina [opened onto the village's main street. Each had three or four main rooms, one behind the other —a front parlor, a main living room, a sleeping area, and a kitchen. There was a cellar for storage and the walls had small niches in which families placed images of household gods.]. At [the pharaoh] Akhenaten's capital at Tell el-Amarna the homes of the administrators were much larger. They were built within a surrounding rectangular enclosure which left space for an open courtyard and a side chapel. The main rooms were decorated with painted plasters. In one house there was a ceiling of brilliant blue, columns of reddish brown, and walls predominantly in white but with a frieze of blue lotus leaves on a green background. Among the comforts enjoyed by the owners were bathrooms, in which the bather stood on a limestone slab and had water poured over him, and shaped stone lavatory seats. There was ample storage space for grain next to a kitchen court at the back of the house. Some wall paintings show houses with ponds and gardens well stocked with a variety of trees. The family could grow its own vegetables. Onions and leeks were particular favourites while the most popular fruits were grapes, figs, and dates. . . .

Such élite homes and their accompanying lifestyle required a mass of domestic help. When a wealthy man went out on business he might be accompanied by two servants. One carried a mat and a fly-whisk, the other a pair of his sandals. His destination reached, the master would have his feet washed, his fresh sandals put on, and then he would settle down on his mat with the flies being flicked from him. Within the home, cooking, cleaning, and waiting at table would be done by servants or by slaves captured in military campaigns.

Social life for the élite was sophisticated. Their homes were furnished elegantly, the furniture carved with animal heads or inlaid with ivory, ebony, or glass. Every care was taken with personal appearance. A box belonging to one Tutu, who lived at the time of the Eighteenth Dynasty, the height of the New Kingdom, was filled with her cosmetics, eye-paint, a mixing palette, an ivory comb, and pink leather sandals. Banquets were an important feature of this lifestyle and they were conducted according to elaborate rituals. The host stood at his gate and was greeted formally by his guests as they arrived. He responded in kind and then led them indoors where both sexes settled down for the meal. Music was an essential part of any feast. Dancing girls would perform to the sound of harps, lutes, oboes, or flutes.

The Lives and Rights of Egyptian Women

Erika Feucht

This discussion of ancient Egyptian women is by Erika Feucht, an Egyptologist at Germany's University of Heidelberg. She covers a wide range of issues, including how women dressed, their relationships with their husbands, their status in both home and society in general, and their rights or lack thereof. Especially revealing is Feucht's comparison of ancient and modern Egyptian women, which comes to the surprising conclusion that ancient women enjoyed a stronger social position than modern ones.

Very few sources give us insight into the life of women in Egypt. Most of them are found on monuments or in wisdom texts, myths, and stories written by men, portraying their point of view. Erected by a privileged class, the monuments give us a glimpse of wives, mothers, and daughters in their relationships with kings, officials, and priests. We must be aware, however, that they merely reflect an ideal life according to the principles of *maat* (personified as a goddess of truth, justice, and world order); the reality of everyday life must have been different. As for the daily life and the rights of women of the lower echelons of society, we have virtually no information for the Old Kingdom period. Only the legal documents and letters on papyrus that are preserved in increasing numbers from the Middle Kingdom onward begin to form a mosaic-like picture, however fragmentary.

No Need to Hide Their Bodies

In the decorations of her husband's tomb, the wife is depicted as an equal, participating in her husband's life on earth as well as in the Hereafter. Not only did she not have to hide her body during any period of Egyptian history, but its charms were even accentuated in wall paintings and reliefs. The male ideal of a

Erika Feucht, "Women," *The Egyptians*, edited by Sergio Donadoni and translated by Roberto Bianchi. Chicago: University of Chicago Press, 1990. Copyright © 1990 by University of Chicago. Reproduced by permission.

woman is expressed in this description of a lover:

> Radiant, white of skin with clear, shining eyes,
> with lips that speak sweetly; she does not say one word too many;
> with a high neck and white breast,
> her hair genuine lapis lazuli.
> Her arms surpass gold,
> her fingers resemble lotus blossoms.
> Her hips full, her waist supple,
> she whose thighs compete for her beauty,
> with noble gait when she treads the earth.

We encounter this image of women in all periods of Egyptian history, but men were occasionally depicted as well-nourished dignitaries with wrinkled bellies, although youthful representations predominate. From the earliest periods until the beginning of the fourteenth century B.C., reliefs and sculptures in the round showed women clad in tight-fitting dresses that were secured with wide shoulder straps and that revealed their slender figures. When the garment became more voluminous, it was not to veil the body but, rather, to accentuate its charms: the flowing, folded or pleated fabric was so sheer that the shape of the body and even the navel were revealed. In contrast to men, who were depicted either with shaven heads or wearing short or long wigs, the women of all periods had long, thick hair that was supplemented, if necessary, by hairpieces of natural hair, vegetable fiber, or later even wool, or replaced by wigs. The eyes of men and women alike were outlined with makeup. It should be noted that the makeup with its antiseptic components like galena (black) or copper oxide (green) also offered protection from trachoma, still common today.

Although this is an ideal image of women as shaped by men, female members of the lower echelons of society were never depicted in a degrading way either, even if they had bared their chests in the heat of a bakery like their male colleagues.

Though Amenophis III had joyfully added two Mitanni princesses to his harem, he refused to send an Egyptian princess to the sovereign of Mitanni, because "from time immemorial a royal daughter from Egypt has been given to no one." This is not only an expression of the feeling of superiority of the Egyptians over the foreigners but at the same time an indication of the solicitude accorded female relatives, who could not be inconvenienced by living among "barbarians."

Women Enjoy Unusual Respect and Freedom

In his tomb Petosiris, who lived through the conquest of Egypt by Alexander the Great, describes his feelings for his wife in the following way:

> His wife, his beloved,
> mistress of amiability, sweet in love,
> clever in conversation, pleasant in her words,
> with excellent counsel in her writings,
> everything that passes her lips is like the work of Maat,
> a perfect woman, highly regarded in her town,
> who lends a hand to everyone and says what is good,
> who repeats what people like to hear, who brings joy to everybody,
> whose lips no evil word passes, very popular everywhere.

The wife of this eminent man, who held a high priestly office in his town, is described as a partner of her husband. Like her husband, she was in contact with the world outside and was able to win the respect of the citizens by her good acts. The occasional statements found in the tombs of men about their wives almost two thousand years earlier, in the latter half of the Sixth Dynasty, are very similar. Besides the usual statements that a wife is "beloved by her husband" or "justified by her husband," there are inscriptions that describe her as "someone who speaks beautifully and loves her husband dearly," as "someone whom people appreciate," or as "someone whom her entire town loves." One man declares: "great was my respect for her. She never uttered a word that was repulsive to my heart, and she was never mean as long as she was youthful in life." These short remarks are surprisingly similar to the later words of Petosiris about his wife. Some of the statements portray a gracious female who makes her husband happy, and some describe her appreciation by her fellow citizens. Twice her actions in the social sphere are characterized in words similar to those of the autobiographical inscriptions of men in which, starting at the end of the Sixth Dynasty, the tomb owner usually emphasizes his concern for the welfare of the poor. The women are called "someone who gives bread to the hungry and clothing to the naked" or "someone who does good things for the heart of the orphan," which is a variation on the common male epithet "he who protects the widow and the orphan."

[The ancient Greek historian] Diodorus Siculus claimed that Egyptian women had power over their husbands. This impression may have arisen among the Greeks who settled in Egypt during the centuries before and after the birth of Christ and who formed a large part of the population of Lower Egypt during the Greco-Roman Period. Unlike Egyptian women, Greek women had to spend all their lives in the privacy of their homes tending

A Deceased Wife Harasses Her Husband

The position of women in Egyptian society was high enough for a dead woman to hold power over a living man. It was a common belief that the spirits of the dead had potent powers and could either help or hinder the living. And people sometimes wrote positive or negative comments and placed them in tombs, expecting that the dead would read them. In this message, a husband pleads with his deceased wife to stop making bad things happen to him.

What wicked thing have I done to thee that I should have come to this evil pass? What have I done to thee?

But what *thou* hast done is to have laid hands on me [caused bad things to happen to me], although I had done nothing wicked to thee. From the time I lived with thee as thy husband down to today, what have I done to thee that I need hide? . . .

When thou didst sicken of the illness which thou hadst, I caused a master-physician to be fetched, and he gave thee treatment, and did everything which thou didst command. And when . . . this condition had befallen thee, I spent eight months without eating and drinking like a man. And . . . [I] wept exceedingly together with my household in front of my street-quarter. And I gave linen clothes to wrap thee, and caused many clothes to be made, and left no benefit undone that had to be performed for thee. And now, behold, I have spent three years alone without entering into a house, though it is not right that one like me should have to do it. This have I done for thy sake.

But behold, thou dost not know good from bad. Therefore judgment shall be made between thee and me.

Quoted in Josephine Mayer and Tom Prideaux, eds., *Never to Die: The Egyptians in Their Own Words.* New York: Viking, 1938, pp. 166–68.

to domestic duties while their husbands not only went about their business outside but socialized with their colleagues and friends, sought out hetaeras [paid companions], and satisfied their sexual desires with prostitutes. Greek women were not allowed to go where they pleased and needed a guardian in legal matters. Egyptian women, on the other hand, led much freer lives and were able to decide their own affairs. Women's seeming liberty to go anywhere prompted [the Greek historian] Herodotus's statement that the Egyptians had reversed the traditions of mankind; women, for instance, went to the market and engaged in commerce while the men stayed at home weaving. Although this was not true for all levels of society, men did, in fact, weave, and women did go to the market and haggled with merchants or sold their own products. Working-class women did not have to be separated from their male colleagues either. In the bakery and the weavers workshop and during the winnowing in the fields, men and women worked side by side.

Evidence for Both Good and Bad Women

A papyrus dating from the second century A.D. states that the goddess Isis granted as much power to women as to men. In the following we will investigate to what extent the ancient Egyptian sources confirm this claim.

A married woman of the middle or upper class probably focused on her duties as a wife and mother; her fair skin, as depicted in paintings, indicates that she spent most of her time inside the house, whereas the husband went about his business outside the house. In the Tale of the Two Brothers, the wife awaits her husband's return from the field, pours water over his hands, and lights a lamp. In a lawsuit about the purchase of a female slave, a woman described how she had moved into the house of her husband and began to weave and sew her clothes. In the seventh year of her marriage, she bought a female slave offered to her by a trader. Her husband was not involved either in this transaction or in the later lawsuit; the wife was perfectly free to act on her own behalf and had full legal standing.

The domestic responsibilities could involve the husband's possessions outside the house. The loving obituary that the Twentieth Dynasty scribe Butehamun of the workers' village of Deir al-

Medina placed in the tomb of his deceased wife, Akhtay, shows that in the family of an official, whose time was taken up by his professional duties, the responsibility for the personal property outdoors was shared by the wife, down to physical labor in the field and the care of the livestock:

> O you beautiful one, without a peer,
> you who brought the cattle home,
> who tended to our fields,
> while all kinds of heavy loads were resting on you,
> although there was no place to put them down . . .

In the Egyptian wisdom texts, the husband is urged to treat his wife well, since happiness and a harmonious marriage depended largely upon his behavior toward his wife. . . .

During the New Kingdom, Ani advises the husband not to nag his wife but to appreciate her value and avoid strife in order to live harmoniously with her. Speaking of "her house" in this context, he underscores that it is her domain as the mistress of the house. A thousand years later, Ankhsheshonqi and the author of the Insinger Papyrus also emphasize the importance of a woman to her husband. A prudent woman with noble character who raises her children well is said to replace worldly riches. The husband should avoid quarrels with his wife and not divorce her, even if she cannot bear children. Ankhsheshonqi's wish "Oh, were the hearts of a woman and her husband far from quarreling" reveals the author's realistic attitude toward marriage. But we also find descriptions of bad women and their effects on the well-being of a man. There are warning against the seductress, who threatens a man, and tales reveal the secret desires and fears of a man who meets such a woman. We hear nothing, however, of the dangers that men can pose to women.

The ideal of marriage as a lifelong companionship is expressed in the New Kingdom in a letter a widower wrote to his deceased wife, by whom he felt threatened. He married her young and remained faithful to her even after his rise in the ranks of the administration. He had not hidden anything from her, nor had he cheated on her like a peasant. He had taken care of her and provided her with everything she needed. Having reached a high position, he had not left as often as he may have wanted. When she fell ill, he summoned the best physician, who treated her according to her wishes. After learning of her death while he was on a journey with the Pharaoh, he had fasted for eight months, and immediately after their return to the Residence in Memphis, he had taken leave in order to mourn her publicly and to bury her with dignity. Even after her death he lived by himself, although that was not right for a man.

The fact that the widower emphasizes his exemplary behavior indicates that not all marriages were so harmonious. The importance of a wife and a family for a man, however, was frequently underscored, and the husband was considered responsible, along with his wife, for a successful marriage. On the other hand, he was supposed to be superior to his wife: Ptahhotep advises him not to give his wife any power, and Ankhsheshonqi recommends that the husband of a young wife (who, by our standards, was still a child when she got married immediately after reaching puberty) form her according to his wishes, keep her financially dependent, and not trust her as he does his mother.

Women were legally protected against physical abuse from their husbands. In a Twentieth Dynasty lawsuit, a man had to swear that he would henceforth refrain from beating his wife, on pain of one hundred blows with a cane and the loss of everything he had acquired together with her.

Men often had to leave their families for months on end: to run administrative errands, attend royal construction works, participate in military campaigns or prospecting expeditions, work on the estates of their lords, or perform compulsory labor. Traveling salesmen fared no better. Men of the lower classes often had to look for work outside their villages and were able to come home only occasionally. Even though the men tried to provide for their wives and children during their absence, the women were largely on their own and were responsible for themselves and their children. They had to take care of everyday problems themselves, although an older son could help them. . . .

Freer than Their Modern Sisters

Summing up the described sources, we can say that although women in ancient Egypt were respected and their legal status was favorable, they certainly did not have the same rights as men. Even though Egypt had a large number of female deities, it is not possible to infer from this . . . that women held a high social position.

Women of all levels of society were largely dependent on the men in their families, although they had their own rights vis-à-vis them. But how many women actually knew their rights or dared to take legal action against one of these men? They lived in the households of their male relatives: their fathers, husbands, sons, or brothers. Only through means given to them by their parents, their husbands, or their children, in rare cases earned by their own efforts, were they able to attain independence. Their opportunities to enter secular and priestly professions were limited, and here, too, they were usually subaltern to men. Even female members of the royal family hardly ever reached top positions. And although women of the ruling class had a high social and religious status compared to the lower echelons of society, with very few exceptions they did not exercise power either. Those few women who held positions of power, however, did so owing to their social context as wife, mother, or daughter of a high-ranking man, and in many cases they wielded this power on behalf of the man (as regent or Divine Spouse). There were exceptions, of course, as there are in any male-dominated society.

In comparing the rights of ancient Egyptian women with those of modern Islamic women, we find a number of parallels, but also differences. As in ancient Egypt, modern Egyptian women are entitled to inherit from their parents. Their share, however, is only half as much as the share of their brothers. In ancient times this share could vary. Since today's marriages are based on a separation of property, women are able to dispose of their possessions independently, as in Pharaonic times. The dowry given by the bride's parents also remains in her possession, even if she is the one filing for divorce. Already known in ancient times, the groom's gift to the bride is a common tradition in modern Egypt. The smaller part is payable to the parents of the bride prior to the wedding in order to cover the cost of the bride's dress and other items; the larger part is due after a divorce. In ancient Egypt the bride received the whole gift herself.

An Islamic woman is entitled to inherit only one-eighth of her husband's property; his children get the rest. The ancient Egyptian marriage contracts show a ratio of 1:2. A Muslim bride can incorporate the right to a divorce in her marriage contract, which is usually done by women who are wealthier than their husbands. If this right is not included in the contract, she can still file for divorce, but she loses all claims on her husband. In ancient Egypt this was the case only if she had committed adultery. However, we do not know the rights of women who failed to draw up marriage contracts.

As in ancient times, the modern Egyptian husband can contractually relinquish his claims to his own possessions for the benefit of his wife and children. Today, as in Pharaonic Egypt, the wife can sue her father or husband on behalf of herself or her children. In contrast to ancient Egyptian women, modern female Egyptian citizens cannot become judges. According to Islamic law, a father can conclude a marriage contract for his son as well as for his daughter. If he is deceased, a male relative, friend, or even stranger has to sign the contract. In ancient Egypt the mother possessed this right as well. In Pharaonic times, the groom negotiated with the father of the bride; women acquired this right in the sixth century. Although nowadays the imam [holy man] can legalize the marriage only with the consent of both partners, many young people, especially in rural areas, do not know this; and even if they do, tradition prohibits a child from opposing his or her father. A child refusing to get married or a woman suing her father or husband is ostracized by society. It is no longer possible to determine today to what extent women in ancient Egypt were subject to similar societal pressures. But some offenses for which women sued their fathers or husbands in the workers' village of Deir al-Medina seem too trivial to risk discrimination by their families or the villagers. The social pressures that subject Muslim women to their husbands even against their rights do not seem to have existed for women in ancient Egypt. Their position was thus stronger than that of their modern sisters.

Love Songs from the New Kingdom

Anonymous

Here, as edited and translated by Yale University scholar William K. Simpson, are nine Egyptian love songs composed during the period modern historians call the New Kingdom (ca. 1550–1069 B.C.). Their content reveals that some were written by men for women, and others by women for men, which suggests that women enjoyed unusual freedom of expression. The passion and earnestness of these poems also suggests that real romantic love (as opposed to the loveless relationships of the arranged marriages so common in various societies, both ancient and modern) existed and may even have been common in Egyptian society. (The numbers of the songs come from an early modern collection of New Kingdom poems by scholar Alfred Hermann.)

2.

My love for you is mixed throughout my body
like [salt] dipped in water,
like a medicine to which gum is added,
like milk shot through [water] . . .

So hurry to see your lady,
like a stallion on the track,
or like a falcon [swooping down] to its papyrus marsh.

Heaven sends down the love of her
as a flame falls in the hay . . .

3.

Distracting is the foliage of my pasture:
[the mouth] of my girl is a lotus bud,
her breasts are mandrake apples,
her arms are [vines],

Anonymous, *The Literature of Ancient Egypt: An Anthology of Stories, Instructions, and Poetry,* edited by William Kelly Simpson, translated by R.O. Faulkner, Edward F. Wente Jr., and William Kelly Simpson. New Haven, CT: Yale University Press, 1973.

[her eyes] are fixed like berries,
her brow a snare of willow,
and I the wild goose!
My [beak] snips [her hair] for bait,
as worms for bait in the trap.

4.

My heart is not yet happy with your love,
my wolf cub, so be lascivious [lustful] unto drunkenness.

Yet I will not leave it unless sticks beat me off
to dally in the Delta marshes
or driven to the land of Khor [Syria-Palestine] with cudgels
    and maces [clubs]
to the land of Kush [Nubia, located directly south of Egypt]
    with palm switches
to the highground with staves
to the lowland with rushes.

So I'll not heed their arguments
to leave off needing you.

5.

I sail downstream in the ferry by the pull of the current,
my bundle of reeds in my arms.
I'll be at Ankh-towy [the city of Memphis],
and say to Ptah [the creator-god of Memphis], the lord of truth,
give me my girl tonight.

The sea is wine,
Ptah its reeds,
Sekhmet its kelp,
the Dew Goddess its buds,
Nefertum its lotus flower. [Nefertum was a deity associated
    with the lotus.]

[Hathor, the Golden Goddess] rejoices
and the land grows bright at her beauty.
For Memphis is a flask of mandrake wine
placed before the good-looking god [i.e., Ptah].

6.

Now I'll lie down inside
and act as if I'm sick.
My neighbors will come in to visit,
and with them my girl.
She'll put the doctors out,
for she's the one to know my hurt.

7.

Back at the farmstead of my girl:
the doorway in the center of the house,
her door left ajar,
her door bolt sprung;
my girl is furious!

If I were made the doorkeeper
I could make her mad at me;
then at least I'd hear her voice when she is angry,
and I'd play the child afraid of her. . . .

13.

Most beautiful youth who ever happened,
I want to take your house as housekeeper;
we are arm in arm,
and love of you goes round and round.

I say to my heart within me in prayer:
if far away from me is my lover tonight,
then I am like someone already in the grave.
Are you not indeed well-being and life?

Joy has come to me through your well-being,
my heart seeks you out.

14.

The voice of the turtledove speaks out. It says:
day breaks, which way are you going?
Lay off, little bird,
must you so scold me?

I found my lover on his bed,
and my heart was sweet to excess.

We said:

I shall never be far away [from] you
while my hand is in your hand,
and I shall stroll with you
in every favorite place.

He set me as first of the girls
and he does not break my heart.

15.

When toward the outer door I set my mind,
lo, the brother [young man] comes to me,
my eyes upon the road, my ears listening,
that I may ambush Pa-mehy [perhaps an imaginary prince
    known for being a lover].

As my sole concern I have set the love of my brother;
for him my heart will not keep silent.

It sent me a messenger,
hurrying on foot,
coming and going,
to tell me he has wronged me.

[In] other words: you have found another,
and she is dazzling in your sight.
But shall the intrigues of another woman
serve to pack me off?

Food and Drink

James F. Romano

Partly because of the richness of the soil in the long green strip of land bordering the Nile, the Egyptians grew a great deal of food and, except for rare occasions, were extremely well fed. James F. Romano, curator of the Egyptian and Middle Eastern departments of the Brooklyn Museum, composed this brief but informative overview of how typical Egyptians stored food, how they cooked, the common meats and vegetables they consumed, their more popular drinks and spices, and what could be expected at banquets given by the well-to-do.

E very Egyptian home had a supply of simple wheel-made pottery used for storing, preparing, and serving food. Grains and other nonperishable commodities were kept in large jars often located in cellars near the kitchen. To guard against petty thievery by servants, wealthy Egyptians would place over the mouth of the storage vessel a pottery saucer that they tied in place by knotting a linen cloth around the jar neck. They covered the knot with a mass of clay or wax stamped with the name of the owner. A would-be thief could not disturb the contents of the jar without first destroying this seal. Strangely, these jars usually have pointed bottoms that prevented them from standing on their own. Representations usually show them leaning against walls or set into simple rings serving as pottery stands.

Most Egyptian homes were equipped with a cylindrical, baked-clay stove about three feet high with a small opening on the bottom to create a draft and to allow for easy collection of ashes. Wood, charcoal, or dried manure, ignited by a simple bow drill, served as fuel. The basic piece of cooking equipment was a two-handled pottery saucepan which the cook placed on the stove. If a stove was not available, the saucepan was balanced on a tripod set over an open fire.

James F. Romano, *Daily Life of the Ancient Egyptians*. Pittsburgh: Carnegie Museum of Natural History, 1990. Copyright © 1990 by the Board of Trustees, Carnegie Institute. Reproduced by permission.

A Wide Variety of Foods

The Egyptians normally ate while sitting on the floor or at low tables. A typical dinner service consisted of a plate, a bowl, and a small mug or jug for liquids. Eating utensils were very rare in ancient Egypt; even members of the royal family ate with their hands.

Under normal circumstances, the ancient Egyptians had as much food to eat as they desired. Only during times of extreme drought or the severest annual inundations was the country unable to feed its populace. The textual and representational evidence suggests that even the humblest peasants could find sufficient nourishment if only through fishing, hunting, fowling, and gathering.

The Egyptians consumed large amounts of meat and fowl. Beef, either boiled or roasted, was eaten regularly by the nobility. Country estate owners kept herds of oxen and cattle that were force-fed until the animals could barely walk; only then were they deemed ready for slaughter. Texts indicate that mutton, pig, and wild game, such as the hyena, were also part of the Egyptians' diet. The ancients raised geese and pigeons for food. They also hunted, killed, and consumed a wide variety of wild birds including herons, pelicans, cranes, and fourteen species of wild ducks and geese. Roast quail was regarded as a particular delicacy. Pelicans were kept as a source of eggs.

Local superstitions prohibited the consumption of certain species of fish in specific locations within Egypt. However, the great abundance of Nile fish proved an invaluable food source for the ancient Egyptians, who delighted in meals of catfish, mullet, bolti, and perch.

The rich soil along the Nile was ideally suited to the cultivation of vegetables and fruits. An Egyptian's meal might have included any number of local tuberous and root vegetables such as beets, sweet onions, radishes, turnips, and garlic. Lettuce was the most popular leafy vegetable. Legumes such as chickpeas, beans, lentils, and peas were also staples. A typical "Egyptian fruitbowl" would have been filled with figs, grapes, raisins, plums, dates, and watermelon.

Every meal had at least a small variety of breadstuffs. The Egyptians made bread from barley and emmer wheat. Their vocabulary contained over forty words for individual types of breads, cakes, and biscuits that specified differences in shape, the manner of baking, the variety of flour, and other ingredients including milk, eggs, fat, butter, honey, and fruit. Perhaps the most popular type of bread was a conical loaf baked in a mold, examples of which appear on representations of offering tables as early as Dynasty I (ca. 3100–2900 B.C.). The importance of bread in the Egyptians' diet exacted a toll on their teeth. Since most flour was ground on grinding stones made of friable rock, small abrasive particles often separated from the stone and combined with the flour. When this mixture was baked and eaten, considerable damage to the teeth resulted.

Beer and Wine

The Egyptians were among the great beer drinkers of antiquity. Their beer had an alcoholic content between 6.2 and 8.1 percent, roughly twice as potent as most modern brews. It was originally drunk from simple pottery tankards. Beginning in the New King-

In preparation for a feast, Egyptian men use siphons to mix several varieties of wines.

dom (ca. 1539–1070 B.C.), however, the Egyptians adopted the Mesopotamian practice of drinking beer through metal tubes. This trend increased the potency of the beer and prevented the accidental drinking of any residual chaff. Ancient texts warn against the abuse of alcohol; to the Egyptians drunkenness was a reprehensible form of behavior.

The frequent depictions of grape arbors on tomb walls and the numerous wine vessels found throughout Egypt testify to the Egyptians' great love of wine. Because of its value, wine was normally limited to the Royal Court and the nobility; if the masses drank wine, they probably enjoyed it only during festivals. Most ancient wine was red, although there is some evidence that the Egyptians drank white wine as well. They recognized superior vintages and labeled wine jars with the year of production.

The Egyptians satisfied their sweet tooth with honey. Salt was used both to flavor and to preserve food. Egyptologists know relatively little about the herbs and spices used in ancient times, but several well known in the modern world—including anise, cinnamon, cumin, dill, fennel, and thyme—may have existed in Pharaonic Egypt.

Banquets

Among the aristocracy, formal banquets provided an opportunity for feasting, drink, music, and conversation. Scantily clad maidens offered guests carefully prepared victuals and drinks and poured water over their hands when necessary. For the occasion, the hosts brought out their most impressive tableware, including finely crafted stone and faience drinking goblets and highly polished metal vessels. Occasionally the celebrants overindulged. Two New Kingdom wall paintings show unfortunate party guests no longer able to hold down their food.

The most elegant banquets always featured a small orchestra. Stringed instruments such as harps, lyres, and lutes were a standard element of any Egyptian musical performance. Both long and short double flutes appear in many orchestral scenes; oboes, trumpets, and an instrument resembling a modern clarinet were also known in antiquity. Percussionists favored drums, tambourines, and small ivory clappers, sometimes carved in the form of human hands.

Sports, Games, and Other Leisure Activities

Jill Kamil

Scholar Jill Kamil, who has published several books about Egyptian culture, wrote this illuminating overview of the major leisure pursuits engaged in by the ancient Egyptians. Included are hunting and fishing, music and dance, swimming and boating, children's games and board games, storytelling, and others.

L eisure was made possible by the economy, exceptional opportunities, and favorable climate of ancient Egypt. Many tombs at Saqqara and Giza contain scenes of the deceased seated with family, friends, or relatives beneath an arbor enjoying the mild north breeze. The panorama of everyday life indicates how vitally conscious the people were of the animal and bird life teeming around them and how much they esteemed outdoor life. It seems that among the greatest pleasures were venturing into the marshes in search of aquatic birds, hunting in the undulating plains of the desert, and fishing in canals and lakes.

Music and Dancing

The ancient Egyptians had a great sense of rhythm and love of music. During important events (such as the breaking of ground by the 'scorpion king,' depicted on his mace-head), a line of women clapped in unison. A piper or singer often entertained fishers and farmers while they worked. And, not surprisingly, we find the wealthy classes enjoying music at all times of day: at their morning toilet, at meals, and during leisure hours. Harps were small and usually played by a seated musician; flutes were in two sizes. A full orchestra comprised two harps and two flutes. Two or three musicians, as well as singers and clappers, often accompanied lithe young women as they performed dances. One such scene, in the tomb of Ti, shows both male and female per-

Jill Kamil, *The Ancient Egyptians: Life in the Old Kingdom*. Cairo: American University in Cairo Press, 1996. Copyright © 1996 by American University in Cairo Press. Reproduced by permission.

formers, who perform separately, each with accompanying hand-clappers. In the tomb of Mehu at Saqqara female dancers raise their arms in a circular motion above their heads while their feet move forward, a gesture probably repeated to the rhythm of the music. A more energetic performance is depicted in the tomb of Ankhmahor, where the dancers do a high kick. In the tomb of Kagemni an acrobatic dance is performed by young girls who are depicted with the left foot placed flat on the floor, torso curved, head dropping backward until the hair, plaited into a pigtail with decoration on the end, hangs down in perfect symmetry. Such scenes, which are commonplace in ancient Egyptian tombs were not, as once supposed, purely for the entertainment of the deceased and their families in the afterlife. They were ceremonial dances, probably suggesting a ritual of rebirth. Music and religion were closely linked. Hathor, for example, the cow-goddess of love and nourishment, was associated with music and dance; her son Ihy became a god of music and patron of the chorus. Hathor's sacred emblem, the sistrum, was an ancient musical instrument that eventually became an architectural feature in temples.

The fact that the ancient Egyptians had no known system of musical notation is somewhat surprising, particularly in view of the development of an independent system of writing at an early date. Perhaps tunes, like the popular stories, were transmitted from generation to generation. We do know that early visitors to Egypt from the Greek mainland around the sixth century BC were particularly impressed with the harmony of Egyptian melodies.

One of the most appealing tales of the Old Kingdom is the story of the pygmy brought from the 'land of Yam' to amuse the young king Pepi II. Pepi was only six years old when he ascended the throne. During the second year of his reign Harkhuf, the nobleman of Elephantine who made many journeys to the south, returned with exotic products and a dancing pygmy as a gift for the king. He sent messengers ahead to inform the Great House, and with great enthusiasm Pepi sent a letter of thanks to Harkhuf requesting him to take every precaution that the pygmy should arrive in Memphis in good condition. Harkhuf was instructed to put trustworthy persons in charge to ensure the pygmy should not fall overboard, and that when he slept guards should sleep on either side of the cabin and make an inspection "ten times a night; for," wrote Harkhuf in his tomb—where he recorded the episode and quoted the king's letter in his biographical text—"my majesty desires to see this pygmy more than all the gifts of Setjru, Irtjet, and Yam."

A legend in the Westcar Papyrus, which relates events in the Old Kingdom, tells of the aged king Senefru's entertainment. A magician recommended that he row on the palace lake in the company of "all the beauties who are in your palace chamber . . . the heart of Your Majesty shall be refreshed at the sight of their rowing as they row up and down. You can see the beautiful fish ponds of your lake, and you can see the beautiful fields around it (and) your heart will be refreshed at this." Senefru forthwith ordered that twenty oars be made of ebony fitted with gold and silver, and that twenty women be brought, "the most beautiful in form, with hair well braided, with firm breasts, not yet having opened up to give birth. Let there be brought to me twenty nets, and let these nets be given to these women when they have taken off their clothes. Then it was done according to all that His Majesty commanded, and they rowed up and down. The heart of His Majesty was happy at the sight of their rowing."

Hunting and Fishing

Outdoor recreations were popular among all classes of society. King Sahure was depicted in his sun temple hunting gazelle, antelope, deer, and other animals, and most nobles' tombs contain scenes showing the pursuit of wild game and capture of various species. The working classes chased gazelle, oryx, wild oxen, hares, and ostrich with equal enthusiasm. Long bow and arrow, lasso, throwing sticks, and bola were the most common hunting weapons. The bow was no more than a meter in length and the arrows, carried in leather quivers, came in several varieties; the one preferred for hunting (which served into the New Kingdom) had an agate arrowhead cemented to a sturdy stick, usually ebony, and fitted into a hollow reed shaft. It was decorated with two feathers and notched for the bowstring.

Considerable ability must have been required in the handling of the throwing stick, numerous specimens of which may be found. They varied in shape. Some were semicircular, others ended in a knob. The bola consisted of a rope or strap about five meters long with a single rounded stone attached to the end. When thrown, the cord would twist round the legs or neck of the animal and hinder its movement. A good hunter could bring down an animal with a careful throw. The noose of the lasso was thrown round the neck of the running victim, whether gazelle, wild goat, or ostrich.

Hunting scenes were extremely spirited, showing the hunter enthusiastically pursuing game in an obvious display of pleasure. Some scenes indicate how bait was used. In Ptahhotep's tomb the muzzle of a young tethered heifer is being seized in the jaws of a lion, which a hunter points out to his two hounds before setting them loose. Hounds were specially trained for hunting and following wounded beasts. Every effort seems to have been made to save the game animals from being hurt and to capture them alive. Ptahhotep is depicted watching men dragging cages containing lion, a frame with gazelles bound together in groups, and smaller cages containing hedgehogs. Sometimes a hunter, perhaps after killing its mother, would take a young gazelle back to the village.

The Egyptians were avid fishers. After the waters of the annual flood receded, ponds were left in the open country. These, as well as the canals and the river, yielded an inexhaustible supply of mullet, catfish, tilapia, perch, barbel, and other varieties of fish. The upper classes penetrated deep into the thickets in their firmly constructed papyrus skiffs, their feet squarely placed on the central plank. They pursued fish with spears—sometimes two-pronged—but never angled. The common folk on the other hand sometimes speared fish like their masters but more often angled from small boats, using as many as five hooks on a single line. Dragnets were drawn from the shore in small canals, trawl nets were used in larger canals and the river, and trap nets were also used. These were wicker baskets with narrow necks, sometimes curving inward; when they were dropped into shallow water, the fish were attracted to the bait and swam inside but could not emerge. Hippopotamus-hunting with spears was popular among all classes. Harpoons were used with great dexterity.

The ancient Egyptians' familiarity with bird life is particularly apparent in the tomb of Ti, where various marsh species are depicted in families near their nests, each drawn with characteristic features and easily identifiable (although not drawn to scale). They include quail, partridge, heron, pelican, turtledove, magpie, swallow, wild duck, and goose. Wading in the reedy swamps near the river are flamingos, pelicans, and cormorants. In fact, indigenous and migratory waterfowl were so plentiful that the ancient Egyptians likened a crowd to a bird pond during the inundation. Birds were most often caught in clap nets. Hunting them with a throw-stick was also an extremely popular sport, which needed skill: the hunter, often accompanied by his wife, children, and servants, had to stand firmly in his boat with legs wide apart and, while maintaining his balance, fling the missile at the fowl as they took to the air. Some of the men with him hold decoy-birds, indicating that the boat made its way quietly through the thickets to creep up on the fowl. Mongooses were trained to catch small aquatic birds, considered a great delicacy.

Swimming, Wrestling, Boating, and Children's Games

It is not surprising, in view of the warm weather and the proximity of the river, that the ancient Egyptians were swimmers from early times. Early Dynastic seals show swimmers in action. It is evident from these and other representations that the crawl was the common stroke. Learning to swim may, indeed, have been necessary training for children among the upper classes, for a biographical inscription of a Middle Kingdom nobleman refers to the encouragement his king gave him and declares that as a youth "he caused me to take swimming lessons along with the royal children."

Confrontation sports like wrestling, boxing, and fencing with sticks were also popular. Ptahhotep's tomb shows wrestling scenes, in which many elements common in Japanese martial arts have been detected. In many tombs the owner is depicted watching boatmen's games, which may have been either an exhibition contest or a race. Light reed boats, often filled with produce, were punted in the same direction, while two or three men stood in each boat equipped with long poles with which they tried to push their opponents into the water. They would then either board the 'enemy' boat or tip it over.

In the tombs of the Old Kingdom, only children (identified by the side-lock of youth) are depicted playing games. Moreover, most of the games are played by boys, and (with few exceptions) boys and girls did not play together. A game requiring skill was played by boys with sharp-pointed sticks, which they raised and threw at a target on the ground between them. A 'tug-of-war' trial of strength was accompanied by such inscriptions as "your arm is much stronger than his," "my team is stronger than yours," and "hold fast, comrades." Boys played a high-jump game, leaping over an obstacle formed by two of their comrades sitting opposite each other with the soles of the feet and tips of the fingers touching.

A girls' game is depicted in Mereruka's tomb: two players in the center hold either two or four partners with outstretched arms; the latter lean outward so that only their heels touch the ground. The text reads "turn around four times." Though there are no reliefs of children playing ball in the Old Kingdom, balls have been found, even in prehistoric graves. Some were covered in leather cut into sections and sewn together and filled with fine straw or reeds. Others were made of wood or clay, in one or more colors. Tops, rattles, and blowpipes, as well as dolls, have also been found. Some dolls seem to have been made by the children themselves from pieces of wood swathed in cloth. They also made toys fashioned of clay: crude human figures and animals like sheep, dogs, tortoises, and lizards, which can be clearly identified. When children died, these 'treasures' were buried with them.

Indoor Games

The ancient Egyptians were also imaginative in their indoor recreation. A favorite game was *senet*, which appears to have been similar to checkers, played on a rectangular board divided into thirty squares in three rows with carved black and white pieces. A large number were found at the tomb of Ptahshepses at Abu Sir. Although the players are depicted facing each other, there is no indication of the rules of the game. The earliest gaming piece (in the shape of a house with a sloping roof) was found in the tomb of the First Dynasty king Den. Predynastic game pieces made of clay coated with wax, along with a checker-board table of unbaked clay held up by four thick, short legs and divided into eighteen squares, have also been found.

A game that appears to have been popular in the Old Kingdom was played with a series of discs about ten centimeters in diameter, made in wood, horn, ivory, stone, or copper. Each had a hole in the center, through which a fifteen-centimeter pointed stick was inserted. We do not know how the game was played. Perhaps the stick was rotated between the palms of the hands to make the discs spin like a top.

Some of the games of the Old Kingdom did survive its fall. One was played on a low table, its surface displaying an engraved or inlaid coiled snake, the head situated at the center of the board and the body divided into transverse lines forming segments. The pieces for this game comprised three lions, three lionesses, and five red-and-white balls; these were kept in an ebony box when the game was not being used.

Storytelling

Storytelling played an important part in the lives of the ancient Egyptians. The deeds of gods and kings were not written in early times and only found their way through oral tradition into the literature of a later date. This treasury of popular tales was based on an ageless tradition in ancient Egypt. . . . The people, their society, and their institutions were molded by the environment and by nature's changeless cycles. The permanence of the physical environment meant that the lives of the rural Egyptians remained stable. While the Great House [i.e., the pharaoh's palace] was striving for political control, and noble fathers were teaching proverbs and behavior to their sons, the life of the peasant farmer was shaped, as in times long past, by the rise and fall of the Nile. Each evening when the sun set, farm work was over. Farmers would put aside their hoes, sickles, and winnowing forks, and sit with their friends in the village or on the rocky outcrop overlooking the valley, and tell tales.

They related all they knew of their ancestors, who, like themselves, knew how to exploit the waters of the Nile. Narmer [or Menes, the first pharaoh], some told, diverted the great river at Memphis through an artificial channel and constructed a moat around the city that was fed by the river. They related tales of the good and kindly king Senefru, who helped the poor; of the wicked Khufu who constructed a mighty tomb in the shape of the sacred *ben-ben* [pyramid], and of Menkaure who was good and just and compensated the poor. Popular and magical tales were closely bound together in a frame narrative, which provided a reason for their telling. Whether or not this was based on propaganda by the central government is not important, once they became part of the stockpile of oral tradition. For example, the Westcar Papyrus relates three stories that mention the names of kings and princes in the Old Kingdom in chronological order. It preserves the undercurrents of what might have been a most inspired, imaginative, and successful campaign to disseminate sun worship. . . . The text reveals that Khufu, builder of the great pyramid, asked his sons to tell him tales of wonders. The first two magical feats recounted took place in the reigns of the Third Dynasty kings Zoser and Nebka, the third in Senefru's reign, and the fourth in Khufu's own reign. The tales end with the prophecy of the imminent birth of three sons by Reddedet, the wife of a . . . priest, who were destined for the throne. The eldest of these children, conceived by the sun-god Re by immaculate conception, would also be High Priest. . . . The purpose of the tale (to show that the kings of the Fifth Dynasty were sons of the sun-god) was preceded by appealing stories of wonder and magic. In this form, it was passed through the generations, becoming part of the oral tradition, until finally set to writing.

The repulsing of Apep, the evil dragon-like creature that lurked on the horizon, was another popular tale. Each evening, at sunset, it tried to stop the passage of the setting sun through the underworld. If the sky was clear, it indicated an easy passage; a blood-red sunset showed a desperate battle between the forces of good and evil; but the sun was the victor and there was always a new dawn. The Egyptians told tales of the world around them: how the sky was held aloft by mountain peaks or pillars that rose above the range that formed the edge of the world; how the sun was a disc of fire that sailed across the heavens in a boat, or was pushed by the beetle, Kheper; how the sky was a mother-goddess, Nut, like the cow that gave nourishment; and how the earth was Geb, who sprouted vegetation, reborn each year as their great ancestor Osiris had been given life after death. They told tales of Osiris who taught them how to produce grain for their nourishment, of Isis his wife who taught them how to weave and grind grain for bread, and of Horus, their son, who was the king who had power over the forces of nature.

They told many tales about their river: how Hapi the Nile-god dwelt in a grotto on an island where the Nile gushed out of the eternal ocean that surrounded the earth, and from where he controlled its flow to Upper and Lower Egypt. They described Hapi as a boatman or fisherman like many of their own, with a narrow belt holding in a large belly and heavy breasts.

And they told tales of their land: how the vegetation that died with the harvest was reborn when the grain sprouted, just as the sun-god 'died' each evening and was reborn the next morning. How Set, the personification of drought, darkness, and evil, secretly aspired to the throne of Osiris, the god of fertility and water. They told how, when Horus was a child and was hidden with his mother Isis in the marshes of the Delta, he was bitten by Set, who had taken the form of a poisonous snake. Isis, in despair, called to the heavens for help, and the 'boat of millions of years' drawing the sun-god across the heavens heard her. Re sent Thoth the moon-god to speak to Isis and offer help. He informed her that the boat of the sun-god would stand still, darkness would reign, there would be no food, and the people of the earth would suffer, until Horus was cured. They told how the evil Set was overcome, Horus became healthy, and the sun-god resumed his journey across the heavens, casting life-giving rays upon the earth and causing the crops to grow again. . . .

[Such stories, along with religious worship, convinced everyday Egyptians that] when they died and were buried on the west bank of the Nile, along with the necessary provisions for the hereafter, they . . . would go to the 'godly west,' where they would live again as on earth. There would be no hunger or want. In this blessed place of peculiar fertility, they would breathe the fresh air along the river banks, fish in the bulrushes, paddle boats along the river, and enjoy fowling and hunting for ever and ever in the 'field of reeds.'

Everyday Rules of Polite Conduct

Ptahhotpe, a royal vizier

An Egyptian was expected to be civil and polite in dealing with others, no matter what social class they belonged to. Thus, just as a peasant was expected to do the bidding of a wealthy person or magistrate (provided the request was proper), a person with power and position was expected to treat less fortunate people with justice and respect. (How often such rules were obeyed or disobeyed is unknown.) The list of everyday rules of politeness excerpted here was attributed to a royal vizier (an administrator who ran the state for the pharaoh) named Ptahhotpe, who lived during the Old Kingdom. But it is likely that he simply wrote down many of the maxims of etiquette that already existed, having evolved in the social sphere over the course of centuries.

1. Do not be arrogant because of your knowledge, but confer with the ignorant man as with the learned, for the limit of skill has not been attained, and there is no craftsman who has (fully) acquired his mastery. / Good speech is more hidden than malachite [a copper-bearing mineral], yet it is found in the possession of women slaves at the millstones. . . .

4. /If you find a disputant arguing, a humble man who is not your equal, do not be aggressive against him in proportion as he is humble; let him alone, that he may confute himself. Do not question him in order to relieve your feelings, do not vent yourself against your opponent, for wretched is he who would destroy him who is poor of understanding; men will do what you wish, and you will defeat him by the disapproval of the magistrates.

5. If you are a leader, controlling the destiny of the masses, seek out every good thing, until there is no fault in your governance. / Truth is great and its effectiveness endures. . . . It is baseness which takes away wealth, and wrongdoing has never

brought its venture safe to port. . . . When the end comes, right-doing endures. That is what a man learns from his father.

6. Do not inspire terror in men, for God also is repelled. . . . No / terror of man has ever been effective; it is (only) the ordinance of God which is effective. Plan to live in peace, and what men give will come of its own accord.

7. If you are one of the guests at the the table of one who is greater than you, accept what he gives when it is set before you. Look at what is before you and do not pierce him / with much staring, for to annoy him is an abomination of the spirit. Do not speak to him until he calls, for no one knows what may be displeasing; speak when he addresses you, and what you say will (then) be pleasing. . . . The eating of bread is under the dispensation of God, and it is (only) the ignorant man who will complain about it. . . .

9. If you cultivate and there is growth in the field, and God puts it into your hand in quantity, do not sate your mouth [do not boast about your good fortune] in the presence of your kindred, for great respect is given to the quiet man. . . .

10. If you are lowly and serve a wealthy man, let all your conduct be good before God. When his former poverty is known to you, do not be arrogant against him because of what you know about his former state; respect him in proportion to what has accrued to him, for property does not come of itself: such is its law for whoever desires it. If it becomes superabundant, men respect him on his own account, for it is God who made him wealthy, and he defends him when he is asleep. . . .

12. If you are a wealthy man, beget a son who will make God well-disposed. If he is straightforward and reverts to your character and takes care of your property in good order, do for him everything good, for he is your son who belongs to what your spirit begot. Do not separate your heart from him, for ill-will makes quarreling. If he errs and disobeys your counsel and defies all that is said and babbles evil words, punish him for all his speeches, show displeasure at them; / it will mean that an impediment is implanted in the body for him. . . .

17. If you are a leader, be pleased when you hear the speech of a petitioner; do not rebuff him until his belly is emptied of what he has planned / to tell you; the victim of wrong prefers

the venting of his feelings to the performance of that for which he has come. As for him who rebuffs petitions, men say: "Why does he reject them?" Not everything about which he has petitioned is what shall come to pass, but a kindly hearing is a soothing of the heart.

18. If you desire to preserve friendship in a home into which you enter, whether as lord or as brother or as friend, at any place into which you enter, beware of approaching the women [making passes at them], / for no good comes to a place where this is done, nor is it clever to reveal them [tell secrets and rumors about them]. . . . As for him who fails by reason of lusting after them, no plan at all will succeed in his hand.

19. If you desire / your conduct to be good, refrain yourself from all kinds of evil. Beware of an act of avarice [greed]; it is a bad and incurable disease. Intimacy is made impossible by it; it alienates fathers and mothers and maternal brothers, it drives wife and husband apart, it is a gathering of all that is evil and a bag of all that is hateful. The man who is exact in right-doing and who walks according to its procedure will long endure; / he will achieve a testament [something to leave to his family] thereby, but there is no tomb for the rapacious [greedy] man. . . .

21. If you are well-to-do and can maintain your household, love your wife in your home according to good custom. Fill her belly, clothe her back; oil is the panacea for her body. / Make her happy while you are alive. . . . Soothe her heart with what has accrued to you; it means that she will continue to dwell in your house. If you repulse her, it means tears. . . .

22. / Propitiate [appease or make happy] your friends with what has accrued to you [with the goods you have collected], that being possible to one whom God favors; as for one who fails to propitiate his friends, men will say that he is a selfish character. No one knows what may happen when he perceives tomorrow, and the straightforward character who is content with it is a (real) character. If occasions of favor arise, it is friends who say "Welcome!" If one cannot bring peace to an abode, one has recourse to friends when there is trouble.

23. / Do not repeat slander; you should not hear it, for it is the result of hot temper. Repeat (only) a matter seen, not what is heard. It should be left alone. . . .

25. If you are powerful and inspire respect of yourself, whether by knowledge or by pleasantness of speech, do not give orders except as concerns business. The quarrelsome man falls into wrongdoing; / do not be haughty, lest he is humiliated; do not keep silence, but beware lest you offend or answer a word with anger. Avert your face, control yourself, and the flames of hot temper will sweep past the pleasant man who is offended and whose path is contested. One who is serious all day will never have a good time, while one who is frivolous all day will never establish a household. . . .

30. If you have become great after your poverty and have achieved property after former need in the city which you know, do not boast of what has accrued to you in the past, do not trust in your riches, which have accrued to you by the gift of God; you will not be subordinate to anyone else to whom the like has happened.

31. Bend your back to your superior, / your steward of the palace; so will your house endure because of its goods, and your payment will be at the proper time. Wretched is he who is in opposition against a superior, for men live only for the season of his leniency. . . . Do not rob / the house of neighbors, do not steal the goods of one who is near you. . . .

34. Be cheerful while you are alive; as for what goes out from the storehouse, it cannot go in (again). It is bread for sharing out / over which men are covetous; he whose belly is empty is the one who complains and he who is in opposition becomes a grumbler. Do not let him be one who is near you; graciousness is a man's memorial in the years which follow the scepter [his death].

35. Know your neighbors while you have property and do not show ill-temper to your friends, it will be a riverbank which fills up; it is greater than its riches, for the property of one may belong to another, but the character of a man of rank will be beneficial to him, and a good reputation / will be a memorial [i.e., friendship is far more important than riches].

Special Skills Essential to Society

CHAPTER

2

Chapter Preface

A special class of highly literate persons called scribes evolved in ancient Egypt. One of the more common writing exercises trainee scribes performed read, "Be a scribe. More effective is a book than a decorated tombstone. . . . [After] a man has perished . . . it is writing that makes him remembered." Scribes had good reason to be proud, for they had mastered a difficult and prestigious skill that few Egyptians ever acquired during the nation's long history. The scribes developed and perpetuated two separate writing systems. The first was hieroglyphics, consisting of small pictures that stood for words and ideas; the second was hieratic, a sort of script made up of straight and curved pen strokes. The scribes also dominated education, dispensing knowledge to members of the upper classes and creating school texts, as well as writing inscriptions, letters, and other documents for the pharaohs and other nobles. Without the special skills of scribes, Egyptian civilization would not have attained the high cultural levels it did.

Yet scribes were not the only members of Egyptian society who acquired special skills that allowed them to make significant strides in cultural areas. Among the other small, highly educated groups whose skills were in high demand were doctors, who compiled a rich and complex tradition of medical lore and knowledge. A good deal of this knowledge was mystical and superstitious in nature. The prevailing wisdom was that disease was inflicted on humans by the gods as a punishment or for some other reason. Yet some doctors, especially in the New Kingdom and the centuries that followed it, began to perceive that at least some sickness had natural, earthly causes and that human doctors could prescribe practical remedies for them.

Another group with special skills—fine craftsmen and artists—also had practicality in mind when they produced objects that combined artistic beauty and everyday usefulness. This achievement is especially evident in the work of metalsmiths, whose gold, silver, copper, and bronze jewelry, dinnerware, figurines, swords, and other artifacts adorned houses, palaces, temples, and tombs. Surviving examples exhibit fine workmanship, particularly when the wares were crafted for royalty. Hundreds of objects made of gold and other metals were discovered in the tomb of the pharaoh Tutankhamen, unearthed in the 1920s; and these remain a testament to the skills and creativity of the more artistic members of a vanished civilization. That they took pride in their work is self-evident. In fact, they may well have believed that "more effective is a well-decorated tomb than a book." But we will never know for sure, for it was the scribes who wrote the words that conveyed the thoughts of the ancient Egyptians to future societies.

Doctors and Their Cures

Adolf Erman

The late German Egyptologist Adolf Erman wrote this informative overview of ancient Egyptian doctors and medicine. For the most part, these physicians had a decidedly imperfect knowledge of anatomy, Erman points out, and conducted their diagnoses in an imprecise manner. Also, most of their medicines and cures were folk remedies, some of which worked, but many of which did not. Nevertheless, over the course of the centuries the country compiled a vast store of medical knowledge, at least some of which was helpful to patients. According to Erman, a few of the ancient remedies were so trusted that they were still in use in Egypt in the twentieth century.

The science of medicine even under the Old [Kingdom] was already in the hands of special physicians called *snu*. We still know the names of some of the royal body-physicians of this time; Sechmetna'e'ônch, the "chief physician of the Pharaoh," served the King Sehurê', while of somewhat earlier date perhaps, are Ra'na'e'ônch the "physician of the Pharaoh," and Nesmenau his chief, the "superintendent of the physicians of the Pharaoh." The priests also of the lioness-headed goddess Sechmet seem to have been famed for their medical wisdom, whilst the son of this goddess, the demigod Imhôtep, was in later times considered to be the creator of medical knowledge. These ancient doctors laid the foundation of all later medicine; even the doctors of the New [Kingdom] do not seem to have improved upon the older conceptions about the construction of the human body. We may be surprised at this, but their anatomical knowledge was very little,—less than we should expect with a people to whom it was an everyday matter to open dead bodies.

Adolf Erman, *Life in Ancient Egypt*. Translated by H.M. Tirard. New York: Dover Publications, Inc., 1971.

Rudimentary Knowledge of Anatomy

Besides the structure of the bones and of the large viscera [internal organs] such as the heart, stomach, spleen, etc., the ancient Egyptians knew barely anything of the human body, and their teaching concerning the *vessels* is mostly characterised by pure invention; this teaching however was considered by them as specially important, it was the "secret of the doctor." These *vessels* correspond essentially with the great veins or indeed preferably with the arteries, but as they thought that they carried water, air, excretory fluids, etc., we must understand their words in a very broad sense, unless we prefer to consider the statements about their activity as pure fancy. The Egyptians realised at any rate that the vessels took their course from the heart to the various members of the body. The heart is the centre, "its vessels lead to all the members; whether the doctor . . . lays his finger on the forehead, on the back of the head, on the hands, on the place of the stomach (?), on the arms, or on the feet, everywhere he meets with the heart (*i.e.* the pulse), because its vessels lead to all the members." The heart was therefore called also the "beginning of all the members." The Egyptians knew little, however, about the position of the various vessels. An ancient manual on this subject declares that there were twelve of them, which went in pairs to the breast, to the legs, to the forehead, and to other exterior parts of the body. In another manual however, more than forty of them are mentioned, some of which lead to the viscera; this manual evidently represents an amended edition of the old teaching; it remains however very doubtful how much is based upon observation. This theory of the vessels is of special importance in Egyptian medicine, for many neuralgic or rheumatic affections were dependent, according to Egyptian ideas, on the vessels. They were stopped up, they were heated, they grew stiff, they itched, they had to be strengthened or pacified, they would not absorb the medicine—troubles which the doctor had to counteract by poultices and ointments.

As a rule the Egyptian doctors thought they could *see,* without further examination, what was the matter with their patients. Many, however, were conscious that an exact knowledge of any disease is the foundation of a cure, and therefore in their writings, directed such straightforward diagnoses as for instance the following: "When thou findest a man who has a swelling in his neck, and who suffers in both his shoulder-blades, as well as in his head, and the backbone of his neck is stiff, and his neck is stiff, so that he is not able to look down upon his belly . . . then say: 'He has a swelling in his neck'; direct him to rub in the ointment of stibium, so that he should immediately become well." Or with one ill in his stomach: "If thou findest a man with constipation . . . with a pale face and beating heart, and dost find, on examining him, that he has a hot heart and a swollen body; that is an ulcer (?) which has arisen from the eating of hot substances. Order something that the heat may be cooled, and his bowels opened, namely, a drink of sweet beer to be poured over dry Neq'aut fruit; this is to be eaten or drunk four times. When that which comes from him looks like small black stones, then say: 'This inflammation departs.' . . . If after thou hast done this thou examinest him and findest that that which he passes resembles beans, on which is dew . . . then say: 'That which was in his stomach has departed.'" Other obstructions in the abdomen gave rise to other symptoms, and required different treatment, thus when the doctor put his fingers on the abdomen and found it "go hither and thither like oil in a skin bottle," or in a case when the patient "vomits and feels very ill," or when the body is "hot and swollen."

Remedies and Cures

If the illness were obstinate, the question arose which was to be employed out of many various remedies, for by the beginning of the New [Kingdom] the number of prescriptions had increased to such an extent, that for some diseases there were frequently a dozen or more remedies, from amongst which the doctor could take his choice. When we examine them more closely, this superfluity of recipes becomes more limited. Some medicines were supposed to act at once, others more slowly but at the same time more surely: "remedies" and "momentary remedies." Many remedies again might only be used at certain seasons of the year. Thus amongst the prescriptions for the eyes, we find one that is only to be employed during the first and second months of the winter, whilst another is to be used during the third and fourth months, and of a third it is expressly stated that its use is allowed during all the three seasons of the year. . . .

There were of course many panaceas [cures] which . . . were said to "drive out the fever of the gods, all death and pain from the limbs of man, so that he immediately becomes well." These wondrous remedies were not invented by human wisdom, but by the various gods for the sun-god Rê', who had to suffer from all kinds of diseases and pain before he withdrew to his heavenly repose. Yet in spite of their supernatural origin, they are composed very much in the same way as the earthly prescriptions. One for instance consists of honey, wax, and fourteen vegetable substances, to be mixed in equal parts; poultices were to be made of the mixture.

Many believed also that the remedy for all ills was to be found in some particular plant, e.g. the tree *Dgam, i.e.* probably the olive tree. In an "ancient book of wisdom for mankind," amongst other things we find the following remarks about this tree: "If the boughs are crushed in water and put upon a head which is ill, it will become well immediately, as if it had never been ill. For the complaint of indigestion (?) let the patient take some of the fruit in beer and the impure moistness will be driven out of his body. For the growth of a woman's hair let the fruit be pounded and kneaded into a lump; the woman must then put it in oil, and anoint her head with it." In spite of these virtues vouched for by *the ancient book,* the tree does not appear to have played a great part in medicine,—we meet with it comparatively seldom in the prescriptions.

By far the greater number of the drugs employed were of vegetable origin; so numerous indeed were the fruits and herbs in use, that a good knowledge of botany was essential to every Egyptian physician. Many plants were indeed so rare that they were unknown to the doctor. The recipe then gives a description like the following: "the herb called *Smut;* it grows on its belly (*i.e.* creeps) like the plant *Q'edet,* it has blossoms like the lotus and its leaves look like white wood."

Plant and Animal Ingredients

Ingredients of animal origin were more rare; amongst these preference seems to have been given to substances most repulsive to us. The idea prevailed in Egyptian as in all folk-medicine, that a remedy ought not to be too simple or too commonplace. A prescription ought if possible to contain many ingredients—there was in fact a poultice which was composed of thirty-five different substances; it was also necessary that the ingredients should be rare and also if possible disgusting. Lizards' blood, the teeth of swine, putrid meat and stinking fat, the moisture from pigs' ears and the milk of a lying-in woman, and a hundred other similar things, were favourite ingredients. . . .

It would not however be right to deny the possibility of results to Egyptian medicine because of this admixture of absurdity. Even with the recipes described above, good cures would be possible supposing that combined with senseless but harmless ingredients they contained even one substance that was efficacious. In many recipes we can discover one such useful ingredient,—as a rule something quite common, like honey, beer, or oil. It would have been sufficient to use that alone, but as no special good result could be expected from anything so commonplace, it was thought better to add to it all manner of possible and impossible things. . . .

The medicine was supposed to enter the *vessels* of the body mentioned above, and this could be effected in various ways, either as a drink, or in the form of pills. . . . Inhalation was also employed; thus in the illness *setyt,* a common complaint of the stomach, the remedy for which was generally warm milk with various additional substances, it was also useful to take the plants *T'e'am* and *'Amamu* in equal parts, "to reduce them to fine powder, to put them on the fire, and to inhale the rising steam through a reed." The following recipe was more complicated but more efficacious; it was to be employed in the same illness:

"The seeds of the sweet woodroof
The seeds of *Mene*
The plant *'A'am*

reduce to powder. Then take seven stones and warm them at the fire. Take one of the same, put some of the remedy on it and put a new pot over it. Knock a piece out of the bottom of the pot and stick a reed into the hole. Put thy mouth to this reed so as to inhale the rising steam. Do the same with the other six stones. Afterwards eat some fat, *e.g.* fat meat or oil."

Eye Infections, Worms, and Fleas

It is particularly interesting to compare the number of recipes in the separate sections of the medical books, for in this way we can judge pretty well of the comparative frequency of the various diseases. The remedies for diseases of the eyes occur so frequently as to form a tenth part of the whole; this shows how common were such complaints. Probably in old times ophthalmia was as prevalent in Egypt as it is at the present day, and as this terrible scourge is now due in great measure to the want of cleanliness amongst the people, we may assume that the same conditions probably existed in old times. The same unwashed children with their eyes discharging, and their faces literally covered with flies, probably formed the same inevitable figure-groups in the street scenes as they do now.

The remedies are also very numerous "to kill worms" or "to drive out the disease which gives rise to worms." The latter expression is due to the singular idea that worms are not the cause but rather the effect, the symptom of the disease. They thought that (in consequence, perhaps, of an obstruction) a gathering formed inside the human body, "which could find no way to discharge; it then became corrupt and was transformed into worms."

The department of women's diseases was of course as extensive in Egypt as it has been and is in all countries, and in addition to the mother, the child at her breast was not forgotten. We learn that from the first cry one could foretell its chance of life; if he cried *ny*, he would live, if he cried *mbe'*, he would die. We learn also how it was possible to tell the goodness of the mother's milk from the smell, and a recipe is given for quieting the immoderate crying of children. The remedy which worked this miracle was a mixture of the seeds of the plant *Shepen*, and of the everlasting fly-dirt; the second ingredient was of course useless, the first may have been most efficacious, especially if the plant *Shepen* was the same as that now used to quiet children in Upper Egypt, viz. the poppy.

We now come to the household remedies, which in Egypt formed a strange appendage to medicine. The doctor was not only required to furnish cosmetics, to colour the hair, to improve the skin, and to beautify the limbs, but people entreated his assistance against house vermin. He was ready to give advice. In order "to drive" fleas, that plague of Egypt, "out of the house," he would order the house to be sprinkled with natron water, or he would cause it to be "properly swept out" with charcoal mixed with the powdered plant *Bebet*. As a protection against fly-stings he might order the fat of the woodpecker, while fresh palm-wine would protect against gnat-stings. A dried fish or a piece of natron, if laid upon a snake's hole, would prevent this dreaded invader of Egyptian houses from venturing out. Supposing however they wished to protect something in the house from the mice, a piece of cat's fat had to be laid upon it, for then the mice would not *approach* it, evidently they were supposed to imagine that the cat was at no great distance. It is more difficult to explain the antipathy which rats were supposed, according to Egyptian belief, to have to the excreta of gazelles. In order to keep these dreaded visitors away from the granaries, they were to take "excreta of gazelles, put it on the fire in the granary, then scour with water the walls and floor where traces of rats were to be seen; the consequence will be that no more corn will be eaten."

I cannot conclude this sketch of Egyptian medicine without referring to one other point.

It is wonderful how faithful the modern inhabitants of Egypt have remained to much of this strange medicine. Centuries have elapsed, the country has passed through the most terrible revolutions, the language is different, the religion has twice been changed, the people have lost all remembrance of their former greatness, but yet they have not forgotten that the excreta of dogs and the bones of fish are excellent remedies. "Against all kinds of witchcraft," the ancient Egyptian employed the following as a good preventive: "a great scarabacus beetle; cut off his head and his wings, boil him, put him in oil, and lay him out. Then cook his head and his wings, put them in snake-fat, boil, and let the patient drink the mixture." When the modern Egyptian wishes to cure haemorrhoids, he takes a black beetle, bakes it in oil, he then removes the wing-cases and the head, and softens them in oil over a gentle fire. It is the same recipe, except that the snake-fat is replaced by ordinary oil.

Case Studies of an Egyptian Doctor

Anonymous

One of the most revealing of the surviving ancient Egyptian medical works (and one of the earliest known scientific documents) is the Edwin Smith Medical Papyrus, dating from about 1600 B.C. Scholars long thought that a military surgeon wrote it; however, recent evidence suggests that the author may have been a doctor who tended to the laborers who built pyramids and other royal monuments. The work is particularly noteworthy in that it largely rejects magic and superstition in favor of observed facts, a sign of a true scientific attitude. Of the forty-eight case studies making up the full text, only one resorts to magical explanations and cures. The four case studies quoted below (from the translation by noted scholar James H. Breasted) cite some serious bone fractures and how a doctor should examine them and employ logical mechanical treatments (such as keeping the patient immobile to facilitate healing). In addition, in the first study, the doctor correctly relates the pulse to blood pumping from the heart to other parts of the body. It must be emphasized that this work is not typical of Egyptian medical literature, most of which remains tied to religion and superstition.

C ASE 1. A WOUND IN THE HEAD PENETRATING TO THE BONE
Examination. If thou examinest a man having a wound in his head, penetrating to the bone of his skull, but not having a gash, thou shouldst palpate [explore by touching] his wound: shouldst thou find his skull uninjured, not having a perforation, a split, or a smash in it.

Diagnosis. Thou shouldst say regarding him: "One having a wound in his head, while his wound does not have two lips, [. . .] nor a gash, although it penetrates to the bone of his head. An ailment which I will treat."

Treatment. Thou shouldst bind it with fresh meat the first day and treat afterward with grease, honey and lint every day until he recovers.

Explanatory Gloss A. As for: "Thou examinest a man," it means counting any one [. . .] like counting things with a bushel. For examining is like one's counting a certain quantity with a bushel, or counting something with the fingers, in order to know [. . .]. It is measuring things . . . in order to know the action of the heart. There are canals in it [the heart] to every member [part of the body]. Now if the priests of Sekhmet or any physician put his hands or his fingers upon the head, upon the back of the head, upon the two hands, upon the pulse, upon the two feet, he measures to the heart, because its vessels are in the back of the head and in the pulse; and because its pulsation is in every vessels of every member. He says "measure" regarding his wound because of the vessels to his head and to the back of his head and to his two feet [. . .] his heart in order to recognize the indications which have arisen therein; meaning to measure it in order to know what is befalling therein.

CASE 4. A GAPING WOUND IN THE HEAD PENETRATING TO THE BONE AND
            SPLITTING THE SKULL

Examination. If thou examinest a man having a gaping wound in his head, penetrating to the bone, and splitting his skull, thou shouldst palpate his wound. Shouldst thou find something disturbing therein under thy fingers, and he shudders exceedingly, while the swelling which is over it protrudes, he discharges blood from both his nostrils and from both his ears, he suffers with stiffness in his neck, so that he is unable to look at his two shoulders and his breast.

Diagnosis. Thou shouldst say regarding him: "One having a gaping wound in his head, penetrating to the bone, and splitting his skull; while he discharges blood from both his nostrils and from both his ears, and he suffers with stiffness in his neck. An ailment with which I will contend."

Treatment. Now when thou findest that the skull of that man is split, thou shouldst not bind him, but moor him at his mooring stakes until the period of his injury passes by. His treatment is sitting. Make for him two supports of brick, until thou knowest he has reached a decisive point. Thou shouldst apply grease to his head, and soften his neck therewith and both his shoulders. Thou shouldst do likewise for every man whom thou findest having a split skull.

Explanatory Gloss A. As for: "Splitting his skull," it means separating shell from shell of his skull, while fragments remain sticking in the flesh of his head, and do not come away.

Explanatory Gloss C. As for: "Until thou knowest he has reached a decisive point," it means until thou knowest whether he will die or he will live; for he is a case of "an ailment with which I will contend."

Explanatory Gloss D [from Case 3]. As for: "Moor him at his mooring stakes," it means putting him on his customary diet, without administering to him a prescription.

CASE 8. COMPOUND COMMINUTED FRACTURE OF THE SKULL DISPLAYING NO
 VISIBLE EXTERNAL INJURY

Examination. If thou examinest a man having a smash of his skull, under the skin of his head, while there is nothing at all upon it, thou shouldst palpate his wound. Shouldst thou find that there is a swelling protruding on the outside of that smash which is in his skull, while his eye is askew because of it, on the side of him having that injury which is in his skull; and he walks shuffling with his sole, on the side of him having that injury which is in his skull.

Diagnosis. Thou shouldst distinguish him from one whom something entering from outside has smitten, but simply as one the head of whose shoulder-fork is not released, as well as one whose nails have fallen into the middle of his hand while he discharges blood from his nostrils and his ears, and he suffers a stiffness in his neck. An ailment not to be treated.

Treatment. His treatment is sitting, until he gains color, and until thou knowest he has reached the decisive point.

Second Examination. Now as soon as thou findest that smash which is in his skull like those corrugations which form on molten copper, and something therein throbbing and fluttering under thy fingers like the weak place of an infant's crown before it knits together—when it has happened there is no throbbing and fluttering under thy fingers, until the brain of his skull is rent open—and he discharges blood from both his nostrils and both his ears, and he suffers with stiffness in his neck.

Second Diagnosis. An ailment not to be treated.

Explanatory Gloss A. As for: "A smash in his skull under the skin of his head, there being no wound at all upon it," it means a smash of the shell of his skull, the flesh of his head being uninjured.

Explanatory Gloss B. As for: "He walks shuffling with his sole," he [the surgeon] is speaking about his walking with his sole dragging, so that it is not easy for him to walk, when it (the sole) is feeble and turned over, while the tips of his toes are contracted to the ball of his sole, and they [the toes] walk fumbling the ground. He [the surgeon] says: "He shuffles," concerning it.

Explanatory Gloss C. As for: "One whom something entering from outside has smitten" on the side of him having this injury, it means one whom something entering from outside presses, on the side of him having this injury.

Explanatory Gloss D. As for: "Something entering from outside," it means the breath of an outside god or death; not the intrusion of something which his flesh engenders.

Explanatory Gloss E. As for: "One the head of whose shoulder-fork is not released, as well as one whose nails have fallen into the middle of his hand," it means that he says: "One to whom the head of his shoulder-fork is not given, and one who does not fall with his nails in the middle of his palm."

CASE 35. A FRACTURE OF THE CLAVICLE

Examination. If thou examinest a man having a break in his collar-bone, and thou shouldst find his collar-bone short and separated from its fellow.

Diagnosis. Thou shouldst say concerning him: "One having a break in his collar-bone. An ailment which I will treat."

Treatment. Thou shouldst place him prostrate on his back, with something folded between his two shoulder-blades; thou shouldst spread out with his two shoulders in order to stretch apart his collar-bone until that break falls into its place. Thou shouldst make for him two splints of linen, and thou shouldst apply one of them both on the inside of his upper arm and the other on the under side of his upper arm. Thou shouldst bind it with *ymrw,* and treat it afterward with honey everyday, until he recovers.

Types and Duties of Egyptian Priests

Ian Shaw and Paul Nicholson

The ancient Egyptians were extremely devout, so it is not surprising that priests played an important role in society and held positions of considerable prestige. In this essay, noted scholars of ancient Egypt, Ian Shaw and Paul Nicholson, explain the different kinds of priests, their duties, and other facts about them.

The Egyptian priest should not be viewed in the same way as a modern religious leader, such as a clergyman, *mullah* or rabbi. The term 'priest' is simply a modern translation for a number of religious offices connected with the Egyptian TEMPLE. The Egyptian priest, literally described as a 'servant of god' (*hem netjer*), was not necessarily well versed in religious doctrine, and, particularly in the Old and Middle Kingdoms, he did not necessarily work full-time for the temple. The common modern translation of *hem netjer* as 'prophet' has led to a certain amount of misunderstanding regarding the role of this official. He was employed at the temple to look after the cult statue of the deity. Like mortals, the god or goddess was thought to have daily needs for food and clothing.

Priestly Duties

Most priests would not have come into contact with the cult image, and, in theory, only the pharaoh, the high priest of every cult, had the privilege of attending the god. In practice, however, his authority was delegated to the chief priest, who was supported by lesser priests who would have attended to offerings and minor parts of the temple ritual. The 'second prophet' attended to much of the economic organization of the temple, while lower ranks, known as *wab* priests ('purifiers') attended to numerous other duties. There was also a female version of the *hem netjer* ti-

Ian Shaw and Paul Nicholson, *The Dictionary of Ancient Egypt*. New York: Harry N. Abrams, Inc., 1995. Copyright © 1995 by the Trustees of the British Museum. Reproduced by permission.

tle (*hemet netjer*) and many élite women of the Old and Middle Kingdoms served as priestesses of the goddess HATHOR.

The chief priest, or 'first prophet', could wield significant power, and this position allowed him great influence in what would now be regarded as secular matters. During the 18th Dynasty (1550–1295 BC) the priesthood of the god AMUN became extremely powerful, and it is possible that they may have been temporarily suppressed in the reign of AKHENATEN (1352–1336 BC). In the 21st Dynasty (1069–945 BC), a succession of Libyan generals took control of the Theban region, using the title High Priest of Amun to legitimate their power.

There were also groups of priests with specialist knowledge, including 'hour priests' whom [noted scholar] Serge Sauneron

---

Herodotus on the Personal Habits of Priests

In this excerpt from his Histories, *the Greek historian Herodotus lists some of the sanitary and dietary habits of the Egyptian priests he encountered while visiting Egypt in the fifth century B.C.*

Elsewhere priests grow their hair long; in Egypt they shave their heads. . . . The priests shave their bodies all over every other day to guard against the presence of lice, or anything else equally unpleasant, while they are about their religious duties; the priests, too, wear linen only, and shoes made from the papyrus plant—these materials, for dress and shoes, being the only ones allowed them. They bath in cold water twice a day and twice every night—and observe innumerable other ceremonies besides. Their life, however, is not by any means all hardship, for they enjoy advantages too: for instance, they are free from all personal expense, having bread made for them out of the sacred grain, and a plentiful daily supply of goose-meat and beef, with wine in addition. Fish they are forbidden to touch; and as for beans, they cannot even bear to look at them, because they imagine they are unclean (in point of fact the Egyptians never sow beans, and even if any happen to grow wild, they will not eat them, either raw or boiled). They do not have a single priest for each god, but a number, of which one is chief-priest, and when a chief-priest dies his son is appointed to succeed him.

Herodotus, *Histories,* trans. Aubrey de Sélincourt. New York: Penguin Books, 1972, pp. 143–44.

interprets as astronomers; he suggests that these men would have determined the time at which FESTIVALS took place. This was an important duty, since the Egyptian CALENDAR was rarely in step with the seasons. Astrologers sometimes determined 'lucky and unlucky' days, and books of these predictions have survived. The HOUSE OF LIFE had its own priestly officials, who attended to the teaching of writing and copied out texts, while it was the 'lector priests' (*hery heb*) who would recite the words of the god. Various CULT SINGERS AND TEMPLE MUSICIANS were needed to accompany the rituals, and women of noble birth, who sometimes held titles such as 'chantress of Amun', were occasionally depicted in this role sometimes holding a SISTRUM [a rattlelike musical instrument]. In the cult of Amun the god was also considered to have an earthly wife, the GOD'S WIFE OF AMUN, which also became an important political title, although the title is not attested before the 18th Dynasty.

Dietary and Sanitary Rules

During the New Kingdom, administrators, in association with the 'second prophet', oversaw the provisioning of the temple from estates and endowments. They ensured that the requisite numbers of offerings were brought in each day, and that the labourers went about their tasks properly. Only the essence of the offerings was thought to be consumed by the god, but the physical substance was consumed by the priests through a process now known as 'reversion of offerings'. Various foods were prohibited by particular temples so that the priests' diet may often have been atypical, but such food TABOOS are common in many religions.

The Greek historian Herodotus states that Egyptian priests were required to wash twice during the day and a further twice during the night, as well as being entirely clean shaven and without body hair. He also says that they were obliged to be circumcised and, since there was no prohibition on marriage, to abstain from sexual intercourse during their period of office. He claims that they were prohibited from the wearing of wool or leather, in favour of fine linen, and that their sandals had to be made from PAPYRUS.

Particular ranks of officials also wore special garments, such as the leopard skin worn by *sem* priests. In addition, there were regulations and prohibitions connected with particular cults. However, although these rules were strict, they applied to individual priests only during three months of the year. This was because the priests were divided into four groups of identical composition. These are now known by the Greek word *phyles*, although the Egyptians called them *saw* ('watches'). Each *phyle* served for only one month before returning to their usual professions for a further three months. Such offices could be very lucrative, in that the priests were granted a fixed portion of temple revenue while in the service of the temple.

Becoming a Priest

Since religious knowledge was not a prerequisite, it is not surprising to find that priests often simply inherited their posts from their fathers, although appointments were also generally endorsed by the king. In certain circumstances, priestly offices could even be purchased, a method that became common under Roman rule. It should be remembered too that in many of the small provincial temples the priests might often have been less important, and the full hierarchy [ladder of authority] may not have been represented. Despite the apparently prosaic methods of entering the priesthood, there was a definite code of ETHICS, including proscriptions against discussing temple rites or practising fraud. The extent to which such codes were actually obeyed is unknown, although cases of malpractice are recorded.

Egyptian Metalsmiths and Their Wares

Lionel Casson

Ancient Egypt had many artisans who produced wares for use by both ordinary Egyptians and the well-to-do classes. Among the most important were the metalsmiths, who turned out cups, bowls, vases, swords and daggers, exquisite jewelry, statues and figurines, and numerous other objects of copper, bronze, and gold, as well as occasionally other metals. This brief but informative tract by noted historian Lionel Casson tells where the smiths got their supplies of metal and how they fashioned them into finely made artifacts, some of which survived the ages and today adorn museum cases across the world.

Until the Middle Kingdom, when bronze finally came into use, smiths perforce made do with copper, fashioning it into tools, weapons, utensils, and, eventually, statuary. Egypt had to import all her copper. Sinai was the earliest source of supply and continued to be important, although from Middle Kingdom times on, when the pharaohs maintained commercial relations with the rest of the eastern Mediterranean, Egypt was able to draw upon the rich deposits in Cyprus. Mining in the Sinai peninsula goes back to perhaps 3000 B.C. For millenniums a steady stream of work gangs, pack donkeys, porters, officials, and others shuttled across the desert that separates it from the Valley of the Nile. It was no easy journey, as we can tell from an eloquent inscription left by an official, the pharaoh's seal-bearer, who had to make it sometime about 1830 B.C.:

> This land was reached in the third month of the second season, although it was not at all the season for coming to this mining area [indeed it was not; the time was close to the beginning of June]. This seal-bearer . . . says to the officials who may come to this mining area at this season: Let not your faces flag because of

it. . . . I came from Egypt with my face flagging. It was difficult, in my experience, to find the skin for it, when the land was burning hot, the highland was in summer, and the mountains branded a blistered skin.

The copper was transported to the shops in Egypt, where it was worked either by hammering or casting. Handles and spouts for jugs were attached with copper rivets. A copper jug discovered a few decades ago reveals that as early as 2700 B.C. Egyptian craftsmen were able to draw copper wire, for the jug's handle, looped over the top, is bound to the neck by wire. One of the most remarkable feats of Egyptian metalworkers is a life-sized statue of Pharaoh Pepi I (about 2325 B.C.) made of pieces of hammered copper riveted together over a core of wood.

From Copper to Bronze

During the Middle Kingdom a transition took place: copper gradually bowed out in favor of bronze [a mixture of copper and tin]. Very likely the change was hastened by the appearance on the scene of the Hyksos [a Near Eastern people who seized control of Lower Egypt for about a century beginning in ca. 1650 B.C.] with their powerful bronze daggers and swords. Bronze, an alloy of copper with some 3 to 16 per cent of tin, has the advantage of being harder, having a lower melting point, and flowing better when heated in crucibles for casting. Though copper was relatively plentiful in the Mediterranean area, tin was not. In a later age, the first millennium B.C. and thereafter, the Phoenicians [a maritime trading people based on the coast of Palestine] sent vessels out into the Atlantic and up to England to bring back shiploads from the rich deposits in Cornwall. For a long while we had no idea where Egypt and the other empires of the ancient Near East got their tin, and some students of the problem were sure that they too imported it all the way from Britain. Assyrian documents of the second millennium B.C. that have recently been deciphered reveal that, beyond any question, the source was the hills of Elam southeast of Babylon. From there the precious metal made its way by caravan to Mari, a commercial center on the upper Euphrates, and was then forwarded to various other centers, including the port of Aleppo in northern Syria, where it was loaded aboard ship for transport to Cyprus,

Crete, and Greece, as well as Egypt.

Iron was not common in Egypt until [the first millennium B.C.]. . . . Some few early objects of iron have been found, but analysis reveals that the metal was of meteoric origin. Among the treasures in Tutankhamen's tomb were an iron dagger and an iron headrest; they were included because of their rareness.

Vast Amount of Gold

One other metal besides copper was widely used in Egypt—gold. Gold occurs in the veins of quartz-bearing rock all along the eastern desert. As early as the First Dynasty it was available in such quantity that in one tomb of the period there were pilasters [pillars set partway into a wall] adorned with strips of embossed sheet gold set no more than one centimeter apart and running from floor to ceiling. The richest deposits, however, were south of the border of Egypt proper, in Nubia and the Sudan. Some was . . . mined along the riverbanks between the Second and Third cataracts, but most was mined from rock, especially in the region southeast of the Second Cataract. Thutmose III was able to bring out of the area no less than ten thousand ounces per year. In the reign of Amenhotep II there is a record of a shipment that needed as many as 150 porters. When the tomb of Tutankhamen was discovered, the world was astonished by the vast amount of gold in it; yet the treasures of this obscure pharaoh who died when very young must have been paltry compared with what went into the tomb of a mighty and aged potentate such as Thutmose III or Amenhotep III.

By the beginning of the third millennium B.C. Egypt's goldsmiths had mastered the working of the metal. They were able to cast it, hammer it, engrave and emboss it, solder it, draw it into wire. They beat it into sheets to cover the handles of weapons or to use on furniture or to be made, as in the case of Tutankhamen, into coffins and face masks. They fashioned it into jewelry, bracelets and necklaces, often set with semiprecious stones such as turquoise, lapis lazuli, and amethyst. [In this way, Egyptian metalsmiths proved themselves to be among the most skilled artisans in history.]

Literacy and Education Dominated by Scribes

H.W.F. Saggs

The vast majority of ancient Egyptians were illiterate. With few exceptions, only well-to-do families could afford to educate their children, so those who could read and write always made up a small and special portion of the population. Such conditions early facilitated the emergence of an elite class of literate men (and perhaps a handful of women) known as scribes, who dominated the field of education and became indispensable to the government, which needed letter writers, census takers, record keepers, and foreign language experts. This overview of Egyptian scribes is by a noted scholar of the ancient Near East, H.W.F. Saggs. He explains how scribes enjoyed an unusually prestigious social position, lists their typical skills and duties, and describes scribal schools, texts, and learning methods.

I n the modern world no skill is more highly valued than literacy. The word 'education' is normally used in the limited sense of literate education; and the percentage of literate citizens has become a yardstick of the social progress of developing countries. In this high, perhaps exaggerated, esteem of literacy, we are reflecting attitudes of the ancient world. In both Babylonia and Egypt literacy was held in honour, and from both regions the scribes have left us self-admiring descriptions of the importance and dignity of the scribal office. Literary proficiency was so highly regarded that even kings claimed it, or had it attributed to them. . . .

A Highly Respected Position

Literacy was a claim . . . made in Egypt, both for high officials and for kings, even before the middle of the third millennium. The chief executive of the Third Dynasty king Zoser, the man responsible for building the Step Pyramid, called himself 'Chief of

H.W.F. Saggs, *Civilization Before Greece and Rome*. New Haven, CT: Yale University Press, 1989. Copyright © 1989 by H.W.F. Saggs. Reproduced by permission.

the King's Scribes'. Sneferu, the first king of the Fourth Dynasty soon after 2600 B.C., was also literate, for a text speaks of him writing on papyrus. A Fifth Dynasty official quotes a letter of commendation which his king had written with his own hand. The third-millennium Pyramid Texts, carved on the tombs of early Egyptian kings to provide for their wellbeing in the after-life, contain further evidence of royal literacy, in spells to ensure that the deceased king, as he entered the afterworld, should be-come the scribe of the god Re; this only made sense if it was taken for granted that kings were literate. From over a millen-nium later, a temple scene at Abydos shows a prince holding a papyrus scroll, and describes him as 'reading out praises'; the prince in question later became the great pharaoh Ramesses II (1290–1224). Scribal equipment figured among the contents of the tomb of Tutankhamun (c. 1340 B.C.), and Ramesses IV made a special boast of having studied all the texts of the House of Life (*pir-ankh*, the academy of the scribes).

To be a scribe in Egypt was to hold a position of respect. High officials, such as a chief magistrate, might be content simply to use the title 'scribe'. A Nineteenth Dynasty text recommends the profession of the scribe, and tells how a man of that kind goes out looking sleek, dressed in white, and finds himself greeted by men of standing.

The high conceit which Egyptian scribes had of the importance of their profession was not without some basis, for the scribal of-fice could open the way to the highest posts in the land. The ear-liest biographical text that we possess is of a Third Dynasty wor-thy, Methen, who tells us that he began his career as chief scribe of a food depot. From that he graduated to become a local gov-ernor and a junior judge. A series of subsequent promotions left him as ruler of a large town, districts in the Delta, parts of the Fayum oasis and one of the nomes, with the final delight of a house covering two acres, set about with trees and orchards and with its own lake.

But not all scribes moved in such exalted circles. In one case it is possible to trace a scribal family from father to son for six generations, and whilst they were men of respectability, admin-istering the people working on the tombs of the New Kingdom kings in the Valley of the Kings near Thebes, they were not of particular distinction. One of them even served as an ordinary workman before succeeding to the office of scribe.

Duties of Scribes

The original creative impulses of the civilizations of Egypt and Mesopotamia did not depend upon writing, but writing quickly followed as one of the consequences of those impulses, and the consolidation and extension of those emerging civilizations rested heavily upon scribal activity. This was not only a matter of recording literature and historical records for posterity; many aspects of those societies could not have operated at all without the services of scribes. Public works and taxation required census lists and other records; the army could not function efficiently without trained personnel to work out its ration requirements; building operations needed scribes to calculate such things as the quantity of earth to be moved, or the amount of stone required and the sizes and shapes to which it was to be cut, or the manpower necessary to move an obelisk: these necessitated instruction in arithmetic and geometry. Communication between the king and his officials, upon which the administration of the state depended, was mainly by letters dictated to scribes; business contracts and court decisions had to be recorded in writing; and international diplomacy required written treaties. An Egyptian scribe might find himself sent on a mission to Syria, and to cope with this he would require a detailed knowledge of the geography of the country. Again, the manifold aspects of religious life—hymns to the gods, prayers and laments, spells and rituals to safeguard against evils—required the services of writing; and the maintenance of the calendar depended upon calculations undertaken by scribes.

In both Mesopotamia and Egypt, scribal training involved a long period of formal education, but our knowledge of details is patchy. [The later Greek historian] Diodorus Siculus transmits a summary of formal education in Egypt in the first century B.C.:

> The priests teach their sons two kinds of writing, that which is called 'sacred' and that which has more general application for information. They devote particular attention to surveying and arithmetic. For the river, by changing the countryside in various ways every year, creates all kinds of disputes about boundaries between neighbours, which are not easy to

sort out accurately except by a surveyor establishing the facts through his expertise.

Some of the assumptions Diodorus makes are questionable. He could be understood to imply that knowledge of Egyptian writing was limited to priests, but this was certainly not the case. He also speaks as though the teaching of writing was exclusively from father to son, whereas it is certain that there were schools where formal teaching took place. However, Diodorus was undoubtedly correct in implying that there was a strong hereditary element in the scribal profession. This hereditary element is reflected in a text, the *Instruction of Ptahhotep*, which describes how the ageing vizier of a king of the Fifth Dynasty, in the twenty-fourth century B.C., set about training his son to succeed him in his office. But this text is concerned with the general behaviour expected of a high official, not with formal education. There is no implication that the son of a high official received no training until his father took him in hand; on the contrary, the duties of the vizier could not have been carried out without a high standard of literacy, and so the text carries the implicit assumption that the son already possessed the basic skills of reading, writing and numeracy before his father began giving him his final polish.

Scribal Schools

In Egypt the scribal craft was predominantly a profession for men, but there are occasional references to female scribes. We also know that princesses learnt to write. We have no precise information about the age at which scribal education began but boys were already attending 'the teaching room' (i.e. school) while they were still heavily dependent upon their mothers. We deduce this from a text called *The Maxims of Ani,* which exhorts a man to be good to his mother because, after suckling him as a baby for three years and clearing up his messes, she then put him to 'the teaching room' where he was taught to write. This suggests an age of perhaps as young as four and certainly not more than six.

In the early stages pupils wrote on the cheapest material available, ostraca, that is potsherds and flakes of limestone. The first stages of writing used the simpler hieratic script, not hieroglyphics. The 'teaching room' was strictly a day school, for we learn that the mother waited at home each day for her young son to give him bread and beer. In the New Kingdom at least, school classes were often held outside, to judge by heaps of ostraca bearing exercises of a few lines each, mostly extracts from three particular compositions. The elementary scribal training lasted for four years, after which the trainee scribe went on to more advanced work. Teachers kept their pupils to their tasks by the sanction of corporal punishment: it was said that 'a lad's ear is on his back and he listens when he is beaten'.

Ancient Egyptian sources give us nothing very specific about schools for older pupils, although we know that some cities contained educational institutions, to which men of substance sent their sons. A Middle Kingdom work called *The Satire on Trades* begins with a man sailing south from the Delta to place his son in the scribal school at Memphis among the sons of notables. Since the principal government departments and temples needed administrators and clerks, it is likely that many of them organized the training of suitable boys for this. When the Persians took Egypt over in the late sixth century, King Darius established academies to train his civil service, in continuation of older Egyptian practice; the text describing this specifically says that he only accepted trainees of good family, but this elitism derived from Persian and not Egyptian attitudes; at earlier periods boys of humble origin could and did become scribes, and in a text from the end of the third millennium a king instructs his son: 'Do not prefer the wellborn to the commoner'.

Copying the Spoken Word

Once settled in their schools, students had to cope with two main tasks: one was to learn certain ancient literary works by heart, and the other was to become competent in writing to a degree at which they could compose letters and official documents. Learning by heart was achieved by the class members reciting aloud in chorus: we have a text which refers to someone's old school friend as 'the man with whom you once used to chant the writings'. Skill in penmanship and drafting documents was acquired by constant practice in writing out texts. . . . In the New Kingdom period (1554–1080 B.C.) the texts used for this purpose were mainly of two kinds. Some were documents of recent origin in the form of specimen letters from one scribe to another, obviously useful as models for the real letters that the trainee scribe might one day be required to compose. The other type of practice material consisted of passages from literary works which had their origin in the Middle Kingdom (beginning of the second millennium), and were in a form of Egyptian which by the time of the New Kingdom was no longer the living tongue. To help the trainee scribe master these, there was instruction in ancient grammar. . . . Some of these literary texts were manifestly designed to heighten the motivation and increase the self-esteem and group solidarity of the trainee scribes. One such composition, known in modern times as *The Satire on Trades* . . . pointed out how happy was the lot of a scribe compared with what manual workers had to endure. . . .

Other compositions, from the late second millennium, set out to discourage pupils from taking up anything but the scribal profession:

> *You set your mind on working in the fields and neglect texts. Do you not consider how things are with the farmer, when the harvest is taxed? Grubs have taken half the corn, the hippopotamus has eaten from what is left. There are mice in the field and the locust swarm has come. Cattle munch and birds steal. . . . What remains to reach the threshing floor, the thieves make off with. . . .*
>
> *But the scribe organizes the work of everyone. For him there are no taxes, for he pays his dues by writings. . . .*

These were amongst the texts from which trainee scribes learnt. We do not know how they most commonly wrote their exercises, whether from dictation, from memory, or by copying from written texts, but the last method was certainly customary for at least one work. The work in question was a composition called *Kemyt,* of which there are many copies, evidently the work of learners. At the time these were written, the usual direction of writing was horizontally from right to left, but despite that every single extant copy of *Kemyt* is set out in vertical columns. Had the students been writing from dictation or memory, some of them would have been sure to lapse into the current direction of writing, even if instructed otherwise. That they invariably used the archaic system of vertical columns can only be because they were copying by sight from master documents set out in that form.

This proof of copying by sight in one case does not mean that dictation was never used as a teaching method. Indeed, it must have been an essential part of the scribe's training. There are many scenes in Egyptian art which show an administrator making decisions about assessment and collection of taxes, with a scribe taking his decisions down; scribes could only have done this if they had learnt the skill of writing direct from the spoken word.

For their writing, the scribal students used red and black pigments applied by means of a reed brush. Various materials were available as writing surfaces. We have already noted that the trainee scribe usually wrote on flakes of limestone or pottery sherds, but for more formal occasions writing boards were available. These were slabs of sycamore up to 20 by 15 inches in size, with a skim coating of gypsum plaster, from which an exercise could be rubbed off to allow reuse. The most expensive and prestigious writing material, papyrus, would only have been available in scroll form to expert scribes, although learners might have been given small pieces for practice.

Learning Foreign Tongues

Major states needed communication with other countries, and this required interpreters. Some Egyptian scribes must certainly have been trained for this; there is little direct evidence from earlier periods, but for the first millennium we know that the Egyptian king Psammetichus sent boys to live with Greek settlers in the Delta to train them as interpreters. We also find mention of the teaching of Egyptian to Nubians, Syrians, and other foreigners. Interpreters accompanied the army, and from the Eighteenth Dynasty, there were Greek interpreters at the Pharaoh's court.

A Schoolbook for Scribes

Nebmare-nakht the Scribe

The scribal schools that thrived in ancient Egypt for thousands of years used actual letters and business and government documents as teaching aids. Students would copy these works over and over, becoming increasingly literate in the process. However, these schools also often produced their own literature in the form of works—in a sense schoolbooks—composed by senior scribes for the benefit of student scribes. Their contents usually followed a formula, consisting first of the teacher's advice to the student, urging him to apply himself diligently; then lavish praise for the scribal profession (along with criticism of other professions); and finally, an encomium (expression of praise and thanks) from student to teacher. The following example, known as the Lansing Papyrus, apparently written by a royal scribe named Nebmare-nakht, dates from the 1100s B.C.

1. Title

[B]eginning of the instruction in letter-writing made by the royal scribe and chief overseer of the cattle of Amen-Re, King of Gods, Nebmare-nakht] for his apprentice, the scribe Wenemdiamun.

2. Praise of the scribe's profession

[The royal scribe] and chief overseer of the cattle of Amen-[Re, King of Gods, Nebmare-nakht speaks to the scribe Wenemdiamun]. [Apply yourself to this] noble profession. "Follower of Thoth" is the good name of him who exercises it. He makes friends with those greater than he. . . . Write with your hand, read with your mouth. Act according to my words. . . . You will find it useful. . . . You will be advanced by your superiors. You will be sent on a mission. . . . Love writing, shun dancing; then you become a worthy official. Do not long for the marsh thicket [i.e., do not waste time with hunting and fishing]. Turn your back on throw stick and chase. By day write with your fingers; recite by night. Befriend the scroll, the palette. It pleases more than wine. Writing for him who knows it is better than all other professions. It pleases more than bread and beer, more than clothing and ointment. It is worth more than an inheritance in Egypt, than a tomb in the west.

3. Advice to the unwilling pupil

Young fellow, how conceited you are! You do not listen when I speak. Your heart is denser than a great obelisk, a hundred cubits high, ten cubits thick. When it is finished and ready for loading, many work gangs draw it. It hears the words of men; it is loaded on a barge. Departing from Yebu it is conveyed, until it comes to rest on its place in Thebes.

So also a cow is bought this year, and it plows the following year. It learns to listen to the herdsman; it only lacks words. Horses brought from the field, they forget their mothers. Yoked they go up and down on all his majesty's errands. They become like those that bore them, that stand in the stable. They do their utmost for fear of a beating.

But though I beat you with every kind of stick, you do not listen. If I knew another way of doing it, I would do it for you, that you might listen. You are a person fit for writing, though you have not yet known a woman. Your heart discerns, your fingers are skilled, your mouth is apt for reciting.

Writing is more enjoyable than enjoying a basket of . . . beans; more enjoyable than a mother's giving birth, when her heart knows no distaste. She is constant in nursing her son; her breast is in his mouth every day. Happy is the heart of him who writes; he is young each day.

4. The idle scribe is worthless

The royal scribe and chief overseer of the cattle of Amen-Re, King of Gods, Nebmare-nakht, speaks to the scribe Wenemdiamun, as follows. You are busy coming and going, and don't think of writing. You resist listening to me; you neglect my teachings.

You are worse than the goose of the shore, that is busy with mischief. It spends the summer destroying the dates, the winter destroying the seed-grain. It spends the balance of the year in pursuit of the cultivators. It does not let seed be cast to the ground without snatching it in its fall. One cannot catch it by snaring. One does not offer it in the temple. The evil, sharpeyed bird that does no work!

You are worse than the desert antelope that lives by running. It spends no day in plowing. Never at all does it tread on the threshing-floor. It lives on the oxen's labor, without entering among them. But though I spend the day telling you "Write," it seems like a plague to you. Writing is very pleasant!

5. All occupations are bad except that of the scribe

See for yourself with your own eye. The occupations lie before you.

The washerman's day is going up, going down. All his limbs are weak, from whitening his neighbors' clothes every day, from washing their linen.

The maker of pots is smeared with soil, like one whose relations have died. His hands, his feet are full of clay; he is like one who lives in the bog.

The cobbler mingles with vats [of oil]. His odor is penetrating. His hands are red with madder, like one who is smeared with blood. He looks behind him for the kite [cow], like one whose flesh is exposed.

The watchman [one who guards and cleans a temple] prepares garlands and polishes vase-stands. He spends a night of toil just as one on whom the sun shines.

The merchants travel downstream and upstream. They are as busy as can be, carrying goods from one town to another. They supply him who has wants. But the tax collectors carry off the gold, that most precious of metals.

The ships' crews from every house (of commerce), they receive their loads. They depart from Egypt for Syria, and each man's god is with him. (But) not one of them says: "We shall see Egypt again!"

The carpenter who is in the shipyard carries the timber and stacks it. If he gives today the output of yesterday, woe to his limbs! The shipwright stands behind him to tell him evil things.

His outworker who is in the fields, his is the toughest of all the jobs. He spends the day loaded with his tools, tied to his tool-box. When he returns home at night, he is loaded with the tool-box and the timbers, his drinking mug, and his whetstones.

The scribe, he alone, records the output of all of them. Take note of it!

6. The misfortunes of the peasant

Let me also expound to you the situation of the peasant, that other tough occupation. [Comes] the inundation and soaks him, he attends to his equipment. By day he cuts his farming tools, by night he twists rope. Even his midday hour he spends on farm labor. He equips himself to go to the field as if he were a warrior. The dried field lies before him; he goes out to get his team. When he has been after the herdsman for many days, he gets his team and comes back with it. He makes for it a place in the field. Comes dawn, he goes to make a start and does not find it in its place. He spends three days searching for it; he finds it in the bog. He finds no hides on them; the jackals have chewed them. He comes out, his garment in his hand, to beg for himself a team.

When he reaches his field he finds it broken up. He spends time cultivating, and the snake is after him. It finishes off the seed as it is cast to the ground. He does not see a green blade. He does three plowings with borrowed grain. His wife has gone down to the merchants and found nothing for barter. Now the scribe lands on the shore. He surveys the harvest. Attendants are behind him with staffs, Nubians with clubs. One says (to him): "Give grain." "There is none." He is beaten savagely. He is bound, thrown in the well, submerged head down. His wife is bound in his presence. His children are in fetters. His neighbors abandon them and flee. When it's over, there's no grain.

If you have any sense, be a scribe. If you have learned about the peasant, you will not be able to be one. Take note of it!

7. Be a scribe

The scribe of the army and commander of the cattle of the house of Amun, Nebmare-nakht, speaks to the scribe Wenem-diamun, as follows. Be a scribe! Your body will be sleek; your hand will be soft. You will not flicker like a flame, like one whose body is feeble. For there is not the bone of a man in you. You are tall and thin. If you lifted a load to carry it, you would stagger, your legs would tremble. You are lacking in strength; you are weak in all your limbs; you are poor in body.

Set your sight on being a scribe; a fine profession that suits you. You call for one; a thousand answer you. You stride freely on the road. You will not be like a hired ox. You are in front of others.

I spend the day instructing you. You do not listen! Your heart is like an empty room. My teachings are not in it. Take their meaning to yourself!

The marsh thicket is before you each day, as a nestling is after its mother. You follow the path of pleasure; you make friends with revellers. You have made your home in the brewery, as one who thirsts for beer. You sit in the parlor with an idler. You hold the writings in contempt. You visit the whore. Do not do these things! What are they for? They are of no use. Take note of it!

8. The scribe does not suffer like the soldier

Furthermore. Look, I instruct you to make you sound; to make you hold the palette freely. To make you become one whom the king trusts; to make you gain entrance to treasury and granary. To make you receive the ship-load at the gate of the granary. To make you issue the offerings on feast days. You are dressed in fine clothes; you own horses. Your boat is on the river; you are supplied with attendants. You stride about inspecting. A mansion is built in your town. You have a powerful office, given you by the king. Male and female slaves are about you. Those who are in the fields grasp your hand, on plots that you have made. Look, I make you into a staff of life! Put the writings in your heart, and you will be protected from all kinds of toil. You will become a worthy official.

Do you not recall the (fate of) the unskilled man? His name is not known. He is ever burdened like an ass carrying in front of the scribe who knows what he is about.

Come, let me tell you the woes of the soldier, and how many are his superiors: the general, the troop-commander, the officer who leads, the standard-bearer, the lieutenant, the scribe, the commander of fifty, and the garrison-captain. They go in and out in the halls of the palace, saying: "Get laborers!" He is awakened at any hour. One is after him as after a donkey. He toils until the Aten [sun's disk] sets in his darkness of night. He is hungry, his belly hurts; he is dead while yet alive. When he receives the grain-ration, having been released from duty, it is not good for grinding.

He is called up for Syria. He may not rest. There are no clothes, no sandals. The weapons of war are assembled at the fortress of Sile. His march is uphill through mountains. He drinks water every third day; it is smelly and tastes of salt. His body is ravaged by illness. The enemy comes, surrounds him with missiles, and life recedes from him. He is told: "Quick, forward, valiant soldier! Win for yourself a good name!" He does not know what he is about. His body is weak, his legs fail him. When victory is won, the captives are handed over to his majesty, to be taken to Egypt. The foreign woman faints on the march; she hangs herself on the soldier's neck. His knapsack drops, another grabs it while he is burdened with the woman. His wife and children are in their vil-lage; he dies and does not reach it. If he comes out alive, he is worn out from marching. Be he at large, be he detained, the sol-dier suffers. If he leaps and joins the deserters, all his people are imprisoned. He dies on the edge of the desert, and there is none to perpetuate his name. He suffers in death as in life. A big sack is brought for him; he does not know his resting place.

Be a scribe, and be spared from soldiering! You call and one says: "Here I am." You are safe from torments. Every man seeks to raise himself up. Take note of it!

9. The pupil wishes to build a mansion for his teacher
Furthermore. (To) the royal scribe and chief overseer of the cattle of Amen-Re, King of Gods, Nebmare-nakht. The scribe Wenemdiamun greets his lord: In life, prosperity, and health! This letter is to inform my lord. Another message to my lord. I grew into a youth at your side. You beat my back; your teaching entered my ear. I am like a pawing horse. Sleep does not enter my heart by day; nor is it upon me at night. (For I say): I will serve my lord just as a slave serves his master.

I shall build a new mansion for you on the ground of your town, with trees (planted) on all its sides. There are stables within it. Its barns are full of barley and emmer, wheat . . . beans, lentils . . . peas, seed-grain . . . produced by the basketful. Your herds abound in draft animals, your cows are pregnant. I will make for you five aruras of cucumber beds to the south.

10. The teacher has built a mansion

Raia [Nebmare-nakht's nickname] has built a beautiful mansion: it lies opposite Edjo. He has built it on the border. It is constructed like a work of eternity. It is planted with trees on all sides. A channel was dug in front of it. The lapping of waves sounds in one's sleep. One does not tire of looking at it. One is gay at its door and drunk in its halls. Handsome doorposts of limestone, carved and chiseled. Beautiful doors, freshly carved. Walls inlaid with lapis lazuli.

Its barns are supplied with grain, are bulging with abundance. Fowl yard and aviary are filled with geese; byres filled with cattle. A bird pool full of geese; horses in the stable. Barges, ferryboats, and new cattle boats are moored at its quay. Young and old, the poor have come to live around it. Your provisions last; there is abundance for all who come to you.

You walk about on new lands and high lands without limit. Their grain is more abundant than the pond water that was there before. Crews land at the quay to make festive the barns with countless heaps for the Lord of Thebes. Its west side is a pond for snaring geese of all kinds, a resort of hunters from the very beginning. One of its ponds has more fish than a lake. . . .

Happiness dwells within. No one says, "If only!" Many stables are around it, and grazing fields for cattle. . . .

The fish are more plentiful than the sands of the shore; one cannot reach the end of them. . . .

11. An encomium of the teacher

You are nimble-handed with the censer, before the Lord of Gods at his every appearance. . . .

You are a noble priest in the House of Ptah, versed in all the mysteries in the House of the Prince.

You are the burial priest of Kamutef, chief seer of Re in Thebes, offerer of his oblations.

You are swift-footed at the Sokar-feast, drawing Egypt's people to your lord with the flail.

You are graceful with the libation vase, pouring, censing, and calling the praises.

You are nimble-handed when you circulate the offerings, foremost in calling the daily praises. . . .

You are wise in planning, skilled in speech; farseeing at all times; what you do succeeds. . . .

You are the good champion of your people; your great meals overflow like Hapy [god of the river's inundation].

You are rich in food, you know how to proffer it, to all whom you love, like a surging sea.

You are a magistrate who is calm, a son of praised ones; loved by all, and praised by the king.

You are a man of high standing since birth; your house overflows with foods.

You are rich in fields, your barns are full; grain clung to you on the day you were born.

You are rich in teams, your sails are bright; your barges on the deep are like jasper.

You are rich in crews skilled in rowing; their shouts please as they carry and load.

You are one weighty of counsel who weighs his answer; since birth you have loathed coarse language.

You are handsome in body, gracious in manner, beloved of all people as much as Hapy.

You are a man of choice words, who is skilled in saying them; all you say is right, you abhor falsehood.

You are one who sits grandly in your house; your servants answer speedily; beer is poured copiously; all who see you rejoice in good cheer.

You serve your lord, you nourish your people; whatever you say soothes the heart.

Preparation for the Afterlife

CHAPTER
3

Chapter Preface

When he visited Egypt in the fifth century B.C., the Greek historian Herodotus observed of the Egyptians: "They are religious in excess, beyond any other nation in the world." Indeed, all ancient Egyptians were devoutly religious, no matter what their wealth or station in life. As Herodotus pointed out in his detailed account of his visit, they worshiped a large number of gods, most of whom were pictured in art with the bodies of humans and the heads of animals. To these gods Egyptians of all walks of life erected statues and temples, prayed, sang hymns, and sacrificed animals and plants.

The Egyptians also believed strongly in the existence of an afterlife in a kingdom overseen by the god Osiris. There, they believed, life would be not only eternal, but also comfortable and carefree. The privilege of reaching the afterlife did not come without cost, however, and part of this cost was to observe a number of time-honored burial traditions. These included mummification if the family could afford it. Herodotus provided a fairly detailed description of the embalming process employed in the country.

The Egyptians believed that the souls of animals could also pass over into the afterlife, so many people mummified pets and other animals. Cats, a particular favorite, were considered special animals and the death of a cat caused people considerable distress. According to Herodotus: "All the inmates of a house where a cat has died a natural death shave their eyebrows," and cats "are embalmed and buried in sacred receptacles." Many of these cat mummies have been discovered by modern excavators.

Among the other examples of religious devotion and preparation for the afterlife included dutifully attending religious festivals honoring the gods. These ceremonies were very formal, yet joyous rather than somber in character. In one such festival, Herodotus wrote, "They come in barges, men and women together, a great number in each boat. On the way, some of the women keep up a continual clatter with castanets and some of the men play flutes, while the rest, both men and women, sing and clap their hands." Another important custom was the placing of food, clothes, tools, and/or other everyday items in the grave or tomb along with the body. The common belief was that a dead person's soul would need these things to sustain itself.

One of the strongest attributes of the Egyptian faith was that it was very democratic. Reaching the afterlife was not a special privilege enjoyed only by the pharaoh, his family, and other nobles who could afford fancy tombs and lots of grave goods. It did not matter whether the burial was expensive or cheap, the tomb large or small, or the grave goods elaborate or simple. As long as the key burial rituals were observed, every person who lived a good life could expect to reach Osiris's realm and achieve immortality. That promise gave hope to the living and comfort to their families when they died. Later, when the worship of Isis and some other Egyptian deities spread beyond Egypt, their promise of immortality after death influenced the beliefs of other faiths, including that of the early Christians; and thereby, a key tenet of ancient Egyptian religion survived, even if indirectly, into modern times.

Religious Festivals: Celebrations of Life and Death

Lynn Meskell

The most outward expressions of religious faith in ancient Egypt, including making offerings to the gods and praying to and for the dead, took place at traditional religious festivals, usually held annually. As explained in this informative tract by Lynn Meskell, a noted scholar of ancient Egypt, such gatherings were also important outlets for people to express their personal feelings (including concerns about sickness, sexuality, and other matters), honor deceased rulers and personal ancestors, socialize, and engage in holiday rituals such as feasting and drinking.

In the New Kingdom people had various avenues through which to access religious experience, primarily through a notable suite of ritual practices. The Ramesside Period was a great age of personal piety, where individuals could access the gods through their perpetual submission. Yet temple life remained the sphere of priests and pharaoh, whereas ordinary people were excluded from the inner spaces. A hierarchy [ascending ladder] of relationships had to be negotiated and maintained. Yet the ritual life of the non-elite was hardly impoverished: they had access to oracles and magical intervention and could make offerings to a host of deities and deceased relatives. . . . Scores of votive stelae and statues [offerings given in fulfillment of vows made to the gods] were . . . deposited in houses, chapels, shrines, or tomb markers, rather than being donated at state temples. But there were other opportunities for ritual participation, such as visiting shrines and presenting votive offerings, partaking in festivals, or employing intercessors to take one's case to the temple. . . .

Events with Many Functions

Festivals provided occasions for a variety of pursuits: ritual, religious, social, sexual, sensory, visceral, and so on. All these domains coexisted as overlapping spheres integrating both the living and the dead. [They were] . . . highly stylized events, where everyday life is transformed into art. . . . Festivals forged social links, as one can imagine for any community. . . . Society was less divided in antiquity, and spheres of life—between households, between work and leisure, between public and private—were less distinct than in modern contexts. As such, festivals acted to produce difference. They had their own codes, moral values, and norms, significantly different from those of actions in other situations: they represented a break with formal decorum. In festival time one could legitimately *follow your heart,* whereas social decorum would traditionally promote keeping the heart under control.

During festival times people are freed from the tedium of daily life. There is a cessation of labor and an unrestrained consumption of the products of labor. People escape into a sensual, intoxicating realm and are transported into a state of elation. . . . Festive events constitute the highlights and crises in the rhythm of the religious life of both community and individual. Festivals are also inflected with narratives of the life course: sowing and harvesting, seasonal festivals, calendrical dates, family festivals, religious events, festivals honoring divine figures, and the commemoration of events. The word for festival, *hb,* was written with the determinative [sign or symbol] for a hut and a dish or bowl. The former was a primitive "tabernacle" or simple temple, the latter was used in purification . . . ceremonies. In the various depictions of festivals, such as the Opet festival shown in the Luxor temple, small, temporary huts are shown sometimes covered in leaves and are often associated with jars, presumably containing beer or wine. Both this festival and the "Beautiful Festival of the Wadi" were held in honor of Amun. . . .

Religious festivals actualized belief; they were not simply social celebrations. They acted in a multiplicity of related spheres. There were festivals of the gods, of the king, and of the dead. . . . The Beautiful Festival of the Wadi was a key example of a festival of the dead, which took place between the harvest and the

Nile flood. In it, the divine boat of Amun traveled from the Kar-
nak temple to the necropolis of Western Thebes. A large procession followed, and living and dead were thought to commune
near the graves, which became *houses of the joy of the heart* on that
occasion. Supposedly the images of deceased individuals were
taken along in the procession and then returned to the grave. On
a smaller scale, a family festival also took place in which the deceased again took part. In this way a link was forged between cel-
ebrating the gods and the dead in a single all-encompassing event.

Offerings of Sexual Objects and Jewelry

The connection between religiosity, ritual experience, and sexuality is most fully articulated in this festival. We should not envisage these as separate or mutually exclusive spheres. Festivals
appear to have been free of moralistic overtones or act of contri-
tion [repentance]. They provided a site for a multitude of de-
lights, desires, memories, adorations, and experiences. Some of
those were intensely personal, sensual, and even sexual. For example, we might posit that votive offerings such as phalli [ob-
jects representing the male sexual organ] were made at festival
time. . . . Couples may have used this moment to invoke bless-
ing on their sexual lives, possibly associating themselves with the
divine couple and their union. . . . By the Twentieth Dynasty
women or couples may have slept at the Hathor shrine on a festival night in the hope of [receiving] a dream from the goddess.
Personal names may give us further insight. Many individuals
bear names connotative of the festival, such as Amenemheb
"Amun-is-in-festival" or Mutemwiya "Mut-is-in-the-carrying-
bark," which may refer to their being born or conceived at this
time. . . . The increase in Ramesside phalli at these shrines, as opposed to the numbers in the Eighteenth Dynasty, suggests that
this mass presentation was a later development perhaps parallel
to the Wadi Festival. Inscriptional evidence demonstrates that a
great variety of people visited Hathor's shrines: high-ranking and
minor officials, artisans, soldiers, priests, and obviously women.

The best-attested festivals of the New Kingdom are those in
the Theban area, in particular the Beautiful Festival of the Wadi,
though the adjective often translated as good or beautiful, *nfrt*,
also has connotations of vitality, perfection, wholeness, and com-

pleteness. Ramesside Period prayers, inscribed in graffiti from Hathor's temple at Deir el Bahri, show that people went to the goddess's shrine at the time of the festival in order to pray for bodily integrity and physical vitality, sometimes enumerated on the level of individual body parts. The festival, whose name evoked completeness and perfection, was an obvious time to ask the gods to bestow bodily health: *They [i.e., the pilgrims to the shrine] are in the favour of Amun-Re, King of the Gods, Mut, Khonsu, and all the gods and goddesses of Thebes. May they (i.e., the gods) give bread to the heart of he who loves them. . . . may they grant favours, may they grant an existence in the favour of men and a body in the presence of the gods. May they grant them eyes to see and legs to walk. May they grant a long life and a vital old age.*

At Hathor shrines such as the Eighteenth Dynasty site at Mirgissa in the Second Cataract, festivals may have been marked by offerings of jewelry, since numerous beads and votive necklaces were found during excavation. One may envisage a priest or priestess coming and collecting the offerings and then replacing the baskets, some of which have been detected archaeologically. The fact that these items of jewelry were personal objects suggests a powerful and intimate link with the goddess. Moreover, at the shrine site of Timna in the Sinai, votives were ritually smashed to signify the handing over from human to deity, attesting to the range of ritual practices occurring at the time. There was a high proportion of female donors in the New Kingdom, although generally tomb paintings tend not to show the religious practices of women but rather focus on male activities. Votive material in the archaeological record, some inscribed with women's names, is one of the only strands of evidence for personal piety. . . .

Food and Drink

Elaborate preparations were made to celebrate the Festival of the Wadi by gathering together the garlands, incense, and other offerings required for various ceremonies. One man requests: *Send me a skin and some paint and some incense; and send us greenery and flowers [on] day 18, because they will pour a libation on day 19.* Textual evidence reinforces the idea that singing, playing tambourines and sistra, and dancing were all part of such festive occasions. The local festival of Amenhotep I was celebrated at least six days each year and was a time for drinking: *the gang rejoiced before him for four solid days of drinking together with their children and their wives.* Drinking was also directly associated with Hathor in her ritual aspect as Lady of Drunkenness. The journal of the necropolis similarly mentions the festival of Sokar-Osiris, which was deemed a free day for the workmen. It was especially celebrated at night. People went about garlanded with onions around their necks and brought offerings to Sokar-Osiris and the deceased. The festival was recorded in texts from the site, as well as by representations in tombs. . . . There were no theatrical performances as such in Egypt, but the calendar of festivals may have linked magic, ritual, intoxication, and a certain amount of personal experience. One text relates that a workman went to drink in the village during four days, over a weekend, suggesting a serious yet sanctioned degree of celebration.

Texts from Deir el Medina provide some insight into the preparations and foodstuffs brought by individuals to festivals or other feasts. One text records some thirty-one women, some identified by the name of their daughter or son, but only three men. Each brought bread loaves of various types, oil, and jars, undoubtedly containing beer. This [probably] represents a feast with people bringing presents, although no actual occasion is specified. A series of similar texts shows women bringing food. . . . In other related texts people bring mats and baskets, while others supply dates, persea fruits, cakes, wooden boxes, and other forms of equipment. Such texts are formulaic, with the name of a person listed and then his/her gift. . . . When a text lists more women, this [might imply] that the celebration is for a woman, but this seems a rather reductive and simplistic reading. These could perhaps be private feasts that involved substantial numbers of people making preparations in a highly ordered and regulated fashion, supported by the act of recording itself. Another possibility is that some of these texts may relate to larger, more formal occasions such as festivals involving the entire community and requiring considerable organization.

Music, Flowers, and the Natural Cycle

Festivities were marked by troupes of female singers with sistra and *menat* necklaces, male singers clapping their hands, and the sound of musical instruments. Bouquets of flowers, which enhanced the visual and aromatic quality of the event, were also brought to the deceased, who could perhaps employ the scent to attain new life. This is reflected linguistically: the word for bouquet or garland, 'nḥ, was phonetically the same as the word for "life." Flowers such as the lotus were used to symbolize life for both the living and the deceased. Banquet scenes in the decorated elite tombs . . . may relate to the Festival of the Wadi, showing feasting to excess and other sensory pleasures. Servants are depicted anointing guests, with women being more often decorated with flowers and funerary cones than their male counterparts. . . . In the banquet scene of Paheri a number of female relatives are shown with their nurses, smelling flowers and receiving bowls containing alcohol. Accompanying the image was written *For your ka, drink to drunkenness, make holiday.* A distant cousin named Nubmehy says to a servant, *Give me eighteen cups of wine, behold I should love (to drink) to drunkenness, my inside is dry as straw.* Tjupu, a female relative says *drink, do not spoil the entertainment, and let the cup come to me.* Tomb scenes such as these probably parallel the activities enjoyed at festivals. Indeed the iconography [visual symbols] of festivals and of funerals has much in common, and the ritual practices of the two may have been comparable. . . . At festivals drinks were raised and participants exhorted *for your ka, drink the good intoxicating drink, celebrate a beautiful day.* The phrase "celebrate a beautiful day" probably links the presence of Hathor at the festival, bestowing great happiness upon the dead.

Later festivals at Edfu and Bubastis were feasts of drunkenness that were simultaneously associated with "roaming in the marshes" and the goddess Hathor. . . . Hathor was specifically associated with the pleasures of drunkenness, and the place of drunkenness could also refer to the temple itself. It resounded with positive qualities rather than negative or moralistic ones, being very different from the Western cultural milieu. For the Egyptians, such sensual states bridged the divide between the divine and human worlds. Smelling lotuses and flowers with mildly narcotic properties would have added to the experience of communing with the dead and the deified: *O my god! O my lotus!* is one line of adoration in the Cairo love poetry.

Cross-culturally, festivals take place in a supranormal time and space in which people experience themselves differently for the period of celebration, whether it be ecstatic experience or sensual/sexual activity. . . . The feast is always related to time—cosmic, biological, or historic. Festivals were linked to moments of crisis, the breaking points in the natural cycle or in the life of human society. Death and revival constituted such moments, as did change and renewal, leading to a more festive perception of the world. . . . During carnivalesque revelry, social hierarchy may have been suspended, and inferiors and superiors may have interacted together: each individual was an indissoluble part of the collectivity. They were each released from the mundane and utilitarian, providing a taste of utopian possibilities. Yet festivals cannot be separated from bodily life, the earth, nature, and the cosmos.

Festivals and funerals were both powerful episodes in the Egyptian life cycle, sharing many of the same symbols, practices, rituals, and paraphernalia. They were transitional moments that served many functions: emotional outpouring, feasting, social interaction, religious observance, and communing with the gods. The *Harper's Song* from the tomb of chief workman Inherkhau at Deir el Medina evinces how those worlds conjoined for the ancient Egyptians.

> *Put ointment and perfumed oils gathered beside you,*
> *and garlands of lotus and mandragora flowers to your breast.*
> *The one who sits beside you is the woman of your heart.*
> *Do not let your heart be angry on account of anything that has happened.*
> *Set song before you, do not recall evil,*
> *the abomination of god.*
> *Concentrate on delights.*
> *Oh righteous one, oh truly just man!*
> *tranquil, kindly, content and calm,*
> *who is joyful and speaks no evil,*
> *give drunkenness to your heart daily,*
> *until that day comes in which there is a landing.*

Hymn to Aten

Akhenaten

The Egyptians sang hymns to their gods during religious festivals and other gatherings in which worship took place. Perhaps
the most famous surviving example is that dedicated to Aten (or
Aton), whom the pharaoh Akhenaten (or Akhenaton) described
as the face of the sun. In the late 1300s B.C., Akhenaten, originally known as Amenhotep IV, spearheaded a religious revolution that sought to replace the old pantheon of gods with just
one—Aten. (These efforts came to nothing; in less than a generation, the priests managed to discredit Akhenaten and reinstate
the old gods.) The hymn, which figures prominently in the cli-
mactic scenes of the 1954 film *The Egyptian,* in which Akhenaten
is a central figure, is often attributed to the maverick or "heretic"
pharaoh; however, it is unknown whether Akhenaten wrote it
himself or had his scribes do it.

You rise in perfection on the horizon of the sky,
living Aten, who started life.
Whenever you are risen, upon the eastern horizon
you fill every land with your perfection.
You are appealing, great, sparkling, high over every land;
your rays hold together the lands as far as everything you have
    made.
Since you are Re, you reach as far as they do,
and you curb them for your beloved son.
Although you are far away, your rays are upon the land;
you are in their faces, yet your departure is not observed.

Whenever you set on the western horizon,
the land is in darkness in the manner of death.
They sleep in a bedroom with heads under the covers,
and one eye does not see another.
If all their possessions which are under their heads were stolen,
they would not know it.

Every lion who comes out of his cave and all the serpents bite,
for darkness is a blanket.
The land is silent now, because he who made them
is at rest on his horizon.

But when day breaks you are risen upon the horizon,
and you shine as the Aten in the daytime.
When you dispel darkness and you give forth your rays
the two lands are in festival,
alert and standing on their feet,
now that you have raised them up.
Their bodies are clean,/and their clothes have been put on;
their arms are lifted in praise at your rising.

The entire land performs its work:
all the cattle are content with their fodder,
trees and plants grow,
birds fly up to their nests,
their wings extended in praise for your Ka [personal life-force].
All the kine [cattle] prance on their feet;
everything which flies up and alights,
they live when you have risen for them.
The barges sail upstream and downstream too,
for every way is open at your rising.
The fishes in the river leap before your face
when your rays are in the sea.

You who have placed seed in woman
and have made sperm into man,
who feeds the son in the womb of his mother,
who quiets him with something to stop his crying;
you are the nurse in the womb,
giving breath to nourish all that has been begotten.
When he comes down from the womb to breathe
on the day he is born,
you open up his mouth completely, and supply his needs.
When the fledgling in the egg speaks in the shell,
you give him air inside it to sustain him.
When you grant him his allotted time to break out from the egg,
he comes out from the egg to cry out at his fulfillment,

and he goes upon his legs when he has come forth from it.

How plentiful it is, what you have made,
although they are hidden from view,
sole god, without another beside you;
you created the earth as you wished,
when you were by yourself, before
mankind, all cattle and kine,
all beings on land, who fare upon their feet,
and all beings in the air, who fly with their wings.

The lands of Khor [Syria-Palestine] and Kush [Nubia, south of
    Egypt]
and the land of Egypt:
you have set every man in his place,
you have allotted their needs,
everyone of them according to his diet,
and his lifetime is counted out.
Tongues are separate in speech,
and their characters / as well;
their skins are different,
for you have differentiated the foreigners.
In the underworld you have made a Nile
that you may bring it forth as you wish
to feed the populace,
since you made them for yourself, their utter master,
growing weary on their account, lord of every land.
For them the Aten of the daytime arises,
great in awesomeness.

All distant lands,
you have made them live,
for you have set a Nile in the sky
that it may descend for them
and make waves upon the mountains like the sea
to irrigate the fields in their towns.
How efficient are your designs,
Lord of eternity:
a Nile in the sky for the foreigners
and all creatures that go upon their feet,

a Nile coming back from the underworld for Egypt.

Your rays give suck to every field:
when you rise they live,
and they grow for you.
You have made the seasons
to bring into being all you have made:
the Winter to cool them,
the Heat that you may be felt.
You have made a far-off heaven
in which to rise
in order to observe everything you have made.
Yet you are alone,
rising in your manifestations as the Living Aten:
appearing, glistening, being afar, coming close;
you make millions of transformations of yourself.
Towns, harbors, fields, roadways, waterways:
every eye beholds you upon them,
for you are the Aten of the daytime on the face of the earth.
When you go forth
every eye [is upon you].
You have created their sight
but not to see (only) the body . . .
which you have made.

You are my desire,
there is no other who knows you
except for your son, Nefer-kheperu-Re Wa-en-Re [Akhenaten's
    personal name],
for you have apprised him of your designs and your power.
The earth came forth into existence by your hand,
and you made it.
When you rise, they live;
when you set, they die.
You are a lifespan in yourself;
one lives by you.
Eyes are/upon your perfection until you set:
all work is put down when you rest in the west.
When (you) rise, (everything) grows
for the King and (for) everyone who hastens on foot,

because you have founded the land
and you have raised them for your son
who has come forth from your body,
the King of Upper and Lower Egypt, the one Living on Maat,
Lord of the Two Lands, Nefer-kheperu-Re Wa-en-Re,
son of Re, the one Living on Maat, Master of Regalia,
the long lived,
and the Foremost Wife of the King, whom he loves,
the Mistress of the Two Lands,
Nefer-nefru-Aten Nefertiti [Akhenaten's wife],
living and young, forever and ever.

A Visitor to Egypt Tells How Bodies Were Embalmed

Herodotus

The Greek historian Herodotus paid an extended visit to Egypt about 450 B.C. and afterward recorded much fascinating and valuable information about the land, its people, and their customs. In this excerpt from his famous history book, he describes how professional embalmers plied their trade, varying the process of creating mummies according to the price the deceased's relatives could afford.

As regards mourning and funerals, when a distinguished man dies all the women of the household plaster their heads and faces with mud, then, leaving the body indoors, perambulate the town with the dead man's female relatives, their dresses fastened with a girdle, and beat their bared breasts. The men too, for their part, follow the same procedure, wearing a girdle and beating themselves like the women. The ceremony over, they take the body to be mummified.

Removing the Internal Organs

Mummification is a distinct profession. The embalmers, when a body is brought to them, produce specimen models in wood, painted to resemble nature, and graded in quality; the best and most expensive kind is said to represent a being whose name I shrink from mentioning in this connexion [Osiris, Egyptian lord of the dead]; the next best is somewhat inferior and cheaper, while the third sort is cheapest of all. After pointing out these differences in quality, they ask which of the three is required, and the kinsmen of the dead man, having agreed upon a price, go away and leave the embalmers to their work. The most perfect

Herodotus, *Herodotus: The Histories*, translated by Aubrey de Sélincourt. New York: Penguin Books, 1972. Copyright © 1972 by A.R. Burn. Reproduced by permission of the publisher.

process is as follows: as much as possible of the brain is extracted
through the nostrils with an iron hook, and what the hook cannot reach is rinsed out with drugs; next the flank is laid open
with a flint knife and the whole contents of the abdomen removed; the cavity is then thoroughly cleansed and washed out,
first with palm wine and again with an infusion of pounded
spices. After that it is filled with pure bruised myrrh, cassia, and
every other aromatic substance with the exception of frankin-
cense, and sewn up again, after which the body is placed in natrum [mineral salts], covered entirely over, for seventy days—
never longer. When this period, which must not be exceeded, is
over, the body is washed and then wrapped from head to foot in
linen cut into strips and smeared on the under side with gum,
which is commonly used by the Egyptians instead of glue. In this
condition the body is given back to the family, who have a
wooden case made, shaped like the human figure, into which it
is put. The case is then sealed up and stored in a sepulchral
chamber [tomb], upright against the wall. When, for reasons of
expense, the second quality is called for, the treatment is different: no incision is made and the intestines are not removed, but
oil of cedar is injected with a syringe into the body through the
anus which is afterwards stopped up to prevent the liquid from
escaping. The body is then pickled in natrum for the prescribed
number of days, on the last of which the oil is drained off. The
effect of it is so powerful that as it leaves the body it brings with
it the stomach and intestines in a liquid state, and as the flesh,
too, is dissolved by the natrum, nothing of the body is left but
the bones and skin. After this treatment it is returned to the family without further fuss.

The third method, used for embalming the bodies of the poor,
is simply to clear out the intestines with a purge and keep the
body seventy days in natrum. It is then given back to the family
to be taken away.

Special Cases

When the wife of a distinguished man dies, or any woman who
happens to be beautiful or well known, her body is not given to
the embalmers immediately, but only after the lapse of three or
four days. This is a precautionary measure to prevent the em-

balmers from violating the corpse, a thing which is said actually to have happened in the case of a woman who had just died. The culprit was given away by one of his fellow workmen. If anyone, either an Egyptian or a foreigner, is found drowned in the river or killed by a crocodile, there is the strongest obligation upon the people of the nearest town to have the body embalmed in the most elaborate manner and buried in a consecrated burial-place; no one is allowed to touch it except the priests of the Nile—not even relatives or friends; the priests alone prepare it for burial with their own hands and place it in the tomb, as if it were something more sacred than the body of a man.

A Dead Pharaoh's Journey into the Sky

Pyramid Texts

To the ancient Egyptians, building a tomb and placing a deceased person inside was not considered to be enough to ensure that the person would reach the afterlife and achieve immortality. Magical words were often inscribed on the inside walls of tombs, especially those of pharaohs and nobles, to make sure their journey into the sky (or more properly, the realm of the dead, overseen by the god Osiris) would be successful. The following example comes from the so-called *Pyramid Texts,* carvings made by priests inside the tombs of several pharaohs between about 2350 and 2150 B.C. (It is likely that this and similar incantations were based on versions dating back into the third millennium B.C.)

I

He that flieth flieth!
He flieth away from you, ye men.
He is no longer in the earth,
He is in the sky.
He rusheth at the sky as a heron.
He hath kissed the sky as a hawk.
He hath leapt skyward as a grasshopper.

II

How happy are they that behold him
Crowned with the head dress of Re [the sun god]!
His apron is upon him as that of Hathor [a sky goddess],
And his plumage is as the plumage of the hawk.
He ascendeth into the sky among his brethren, the gods.

Egyptians prepare a burial chamber to help ensure that the pharaoh's journey into the afterlife is successful.

III

Thou hast thine heart, Osiris;
Thou hast thy feet, Osiris;
Thou hast thine arm, Osiris.

He hath his own heart;
He hath his own feet;
He hath his own arm.

A ramp to the sky is built for him
That he may go up to the sky thereon.
He goeth up upon the smoke
Of the great exhalation.
He flieth as a bird,
And he settleth as a beetle
On an empty seat on the ship of Re.
"Stand up, get thee forth, that he may sit in thy seat."

He roweth in the sky in thy ship, O Re!
And he cometh to the land in thy ship, O Re!
When thou ascendest out of the horizon,
He is there with his staff in his hand,
The navigator of thy ship, O Re!

IV

Wake up, Judge!
Thoth [god of knowledge and writing], arise!
Awake, sleepers!
Bestir you, ye that are in Kenset,
Before the great bittern [a large wading bird]
That hath risen up out of the Nile,
And the jackal-god
That hath come forth from the tamarisk [small tree with red
    flowers].

Ye twain that voyage over the sky, Re and Thoth,
Take him unto you to be with you,
That he may eat of that whereof ye eat,
That he may drink of that whereof ye drink,
That he may dwell there where ye dwell,
That he may be strong in that where ye are strong,
That he may voyage there where ye voyage.
His victuals are with you, ye gods,
And his water is of wine, like that of Re.

V

He hath gone up into the sky
And hath found Re,
Who standeth up when he draweth nigh unto him.
He sitteth down beside him,
For Re suffereth him not to seat himself on the ground,
Knowing that he is greater than Re.
He hath taken his stand with Re
In the northern part of the sky,
And hath seized the Two Lands [i.e., Egypt] like a king.

Mummifying Pets and Other Animals

Bob Brier

Many ancient Egyptians kept pets, including cats, dogs, and monkeys, and they routinely mummified these and many other kinds of animals. Citing the ancient Greek writers Herodotus and Plutarch, Long Island University scholar Bob Brier describes this unusual practice, giving several colorful examples and exploring the reasons for it.

The ancient Egyptians mummified all kinds of animals, from bulls to mice, literally by the millions. This seemingly strange practice fascinated both ancient and modern writers, but most of them misunderstood it, assuming that there was a single reason for animal mummification, while in fact there were four distinct purposes: 1) Pets were buried out of fondness; 2) Animals were buried as food for deceased humans; 3) Animals were ritually killed and mummified as offerings to the gods; and 4) Certain sacred animals were mummified when they died of natural causes. Perhaps the most misunderstood situations are those where animals are found in human tombs.

The Importance of Pets

The Egyptians were fond of animals, frequently depicting household pets in paintings and reliefs on their tomb walls. The pet-beneath-the-chair motif shows the master of the house seated with a pet cat beneath his chair. Dogs and monkeys were also frequently shown as pets. Because the Egyptians believed that the next world was a continuation of this one, and that you could "take it with you," it is not surprising that they had their pets mummified and included them in their tombs.

Several animals were found in the Deir el Bahri cache, almost certainly pets. One, a gazelle, was encased in a wooden coffin in the shape of its body, but another pet proved to be a surprise. Within a coffin containing Queen Makare of the Twenty-first Dynasty was a wrapped bundle. An inscription on the coffin suggested it was Princess Mutemhet, and Maspero poignantly conjectured that "The Queen Makare, wife of the High-Priest and King, Pinedjem I, died, giving to the world the infant which was buried with her." The mummy remains wrapped, listed in Smith's *Catalogue General* volume *The Royal Mummies* as a princess. However, when the princess was X-rayed in 1968, she turned out to be a female baboon. Maspero had misread the inscription; "Mutemhet" was merely one of the queen's own names, the baboon almost certainly her pet. The gazelle in the Deir el Bahri cache belonged to her half-sister, Esemkhet.

Describing the death of pets in Egypt, Herodotus says:

> All the inhabitants of a house where a cat has died a natural death, shave their eyebrows, and when a dog dies they shave the whole body including the head. Cats which have died are taken to Bubastis, where they are embalmed and buried in sacred receptacles; dogs are buried in sacred burial places in the cities where they belong.

As we shall see, Herodotus has conflated two different kinds of animal mummies: pets, and those given as offerings to the gods.

Herodotus was not the only traveler to be confused about animal mummies. Belzoni, the Italian strongman turned archaeologist, discovered a cache of animal mummies while he was excavating in the area of the Valley of the Kings in 1816. Not sure of their purpose, all he could do was describe them:

> I must not omit, that among these tombs we saw some which contained the mummies of animals intermixed with human bodies. There were bulls, cows, sheep, monkeys, foxes, bats, crocodiles, fishes, and birds, in them: idols often occur; and one tomb was filled with nothing but cats, carefully folded in red and white linen, the head covered with a mask representing the cat, and made of the same linen. I have opened all these sorts of animals. Of the bull, the calf and the sheep, there is no part but the head which is covered with linen, and the horns projecting out of the cloth; the rest of the body being represented by two pieces of wood, eighteen inches wide and three feet long, in an horizontal direction, at the end of which was another, placed perpendicularly, two feet high, to form the breast of the animal. The calves and sheep are of the same structure, and large in proportion to the bulls. The monkey is in its full form, in a sitting posture. The fox is squeezed up by the bandages, but in some measure the

shape of the head is kept perfect. The crocodile is left in its own shape, and after being well bound with linen, the eyes and mouth are painted on this covering. The birds are squeezed together, and lose their shape except the ibis, which is found like a fowl ready to be cooked, and bound round with linen, like all the rest.

Belzoni knew the Valley of the Kings contained tombs for kings, tombs for queens, and even some for commoners, but he didn't realize that there were even tombs for pets.

A Tomb Filled with Animals

In January 1906, Theodore Davis came upon a pit tomb that surprised him. The tomb lay at the bottom of a twelve-foot shaft cut into the bedrock. Davis described his descent into the tomb in his usual colorful style:

I went down the shaft and entered the chamber, which proved to be extremely hot and too low for comfort. I was startled by seeing very near me a yellow dog of ordinary size standing on his feet, his short tail curled over his back, and his eyes open. Within a few inches of his nose sat a monkey in quite perfect condition; for an instant I thought that they were alive, but I soon saw that they had been mummified, and that they had been unwrapped in ancient times by robbers. Evidently they had taken a fragment of the wooden monkey-box on which they seated the monkey to keep him upright, and then they stood the dog on his feet so near the monkey, that his nose nearly touched him. . . . I am quite sure the robbers arranged the group for their amusement. However this may be, it can fairly be said to be a joke 3000 years old.

Because the tomb is near that of Amenhotep II, Davis suggested that these animals were the king's pets. They could equally well have been the pets of the original owner of the tomb, whoever he may have been.

Near this tomb waited another that Davis' excavator, Edward Ayrton, described as " . . . completely filled with animals, all of which had been originally mummified and done up in cloth wrappings." Ayrton's description of the contents is minimal, but sufficient to show that the tomb housed some strange occupants. One mummy was of a large . . . ape wearing a necklace of blue disc beads; another was of a large monkey whose wrappings had been torn from its head; there were also an unwrapped ibis, three mummified ducks, and " . . . some bundles of intestines made up in the form of little human figures; one of these had near it a mask of beautifully colored stucco, representing a human head, which had probably originally fitted it. This was certainly of the XVIIIth Dynasty."

The contents of the tomb do not make much sense. While all were animals, they were not all buried in the tomb for the same reason. Monkeys, ibises, and baboons were associated with various gods, ducks were not. Ducks were eaten, the other animals were not. . . .

Examining Animal Mummies

Fortunately, many animal mummies brought to Europe and America as souvenirs by nineteenth-century travelers are still available for study. Over the past twenty years my Egyptology classes have performed a series of autopsies on animal mummies to determine the methods used to embalm them. The first mummy studied was a cat, but this proved too emotional for the "cat people" in the class, so all subsequent autopsies were on fish mummies, to which students seem not so attached.

Hundreds of fish mummies have been found, but it is not known for certain *why* they were mummified. Most of the fish mummies are Nile perch, *Lates niloticus*. A painting in the tomb of Khabekhnet, a son of Sennedjem, shows a *Lates* being mummified by Anubis. While we do not know why this species was mummified, we may well know the reason for mummifying a different species, the *Bagrus bayad*. Plutarch tells us that when [the god] Osiris was cut into pieces by his evil brother Set, his phallus was thrown into the Nile and eaten by three fish of different species. One he calls the "Phagrus," which is probably our *Bagrus*. Thus, this fish may have been sacred because of its association with Osiris and perhaps was mummified for this reason.

Our autopsies on several examples of the *Bagrus* showed minimal concern for preservation. In almost all cases the fish were in poor condition, with little soft tissue remaining. It seems as if these fish did not have their internal organs removed and were only partially dehydrated, if at all. As a result, upon burial insects began to destroy the soft tissue. As is often the case, shoddy embalmers' work was covered by careful wrapping, with eyes and mouths beautifully painted on the linen. Our results suggested that mummified animals did not receive anything near the care that human mummies received.

Often confused with mummified animals are foodstuffs provided for the *ka* (soul) of the deceased, to sustain him until he enters the next world. All kinds of foods have been found in tombs, including breads, fruits, meats, and fowl. Tutankhamen's tomb contained numerous duck- and egg-shaped wooden boxes, painted white, that held joints of meat and fowl. These are not mummified, but rather food placed in coffin-like boxes to sustain the deceased.

Were Animals Worshipped?

Most animal mummies played a role in the religion of the ancient Egyptians, but it is difficult to say exactly what that role was. The main question is whether or not the Egyptians worshipped these animals. Most Greek and Roman sources say that they did, while most Egyptologists today say that they did not. The evidence for both sides is worth considering.

Egyptologists generally agree that animals were not considered divine by the Egyptians, although some deities were represented in animal form. For example, cats were associated in some way with Bast, a feline goddess depicted as a cat, but the ordinary pet cat was not treated as a goddess. To strengthen their position, Egyptologists point out that animals such as cats, ibises, falcons, etc., were raised just to be killed and presented as offerings to the gods. Surely animals raised for slaughter could not have been considered gods. This is a reasonable position, but it still does not prove that the Egyptians never worshipped animals. There is considerable ancient evidence to the contrary.

Certainly the ordinary house cat, or its feline relatives raised for ritual slaughter, were not considered gods. The Egyptians understood that there was just one goddess, Bast, not thousands of them mewing and chasing mice. However, compelling evidence suggests that the Egyptians did worship bulls. This evidence was provided first by ancient Greek writers, and later confirmed more dramatically by Auguste Mariette's first excavation in Egypt.

Secrets of the
Royal Tombs

Chapter Preface

In a popular tale that originated in Egypt's Middle Kingdom, a government official named Sinuhe went into exile; but later the pharaoh recalled him and gave him a splendid gift, an honor usually granted only to people of royal or noble rank. "There was constructed for me," Sinuhe said, "a pyramid-tomb of stone in the midst of the pyramid-tombs." This tomb, if it ever existed, was far smaller and more modest than the great pyramids erected earlier for some of the kings of the Old Kingdom. Indeed, perhaps no other aspect of ancient Egyptian culture has captured the imagination of the modern world more than the giant pyramids that were listed among the seven wonders of the ancient world and still tower over the landscape at Giza, near modern Cairo.

The main chambers within these monuments were originally filled with grave goods, including fine works of art. Even the non-noble Sinuhe saw a statue "overlaid with gold" placed in his little pyramid. Not surprisingly, the grave goods in the royal pyramids were considerably more numerous and lavish. Unfortunately, grave robbers looted these treasures in ancient times; and it was not long before the dark and winding corridors within the largest tomb of all—the Great Pyramid of Khufu—led to an empty, lonely chamber. Yet in later centuries people began to explore the passages in the structure simply out of curiosity for the mysterious and quaint.

For a long time the modern world focused on the wonders of the pyramids themselves and paid little attention to their builders. In time, though, it became clear that the workers were not slaves, as portrayed so often in the movies, but free Egyptians. In his description of his own modest pyramid, Sinuhe mentions "stone-masons who hew a pyramid-tomb," "draftsmen," "sculptors," and "overseers" of the laborers who lifted the stones. Where did these workers live and how did they sustain themselves during the many years it took to raise Khufu's tomb? Only in the last years of the twentieth century did the remnants of a workers' city begin to emerge from the sands near the Giza pyramid complex, a settlement with houses, storehouses, bakeries, food-processing facilities, and much more.

The giant tombs these workers erected were extremely expensive and time-consuming to build, so they eventually went out of fashion. In hopes of escaping the grave robbers, most of the later pharaohs, along with their collections of valuable grave goods, were buried in small secret tombs carved out of rocky hillsides. However, nearly all of these tombs were looted, too, over the centuries. One major exception came to light in the 1920s, when archaeologist Howard Carter unearthed the largely intact tomb of the pharaoh Tutankhamen, whom the modern world came to call "King Tut." The fabulous treasures found in this tomb continue to fascinate scholars and ordinary people alike, helping to keep interest in the ancient Egyptians' long dead culture alive and strong. Meanwhile, the surviving tombs, along with surviving written tracts like the story of Sinuhe, serve as reminders of the great amount of respect and care the Egyptians invested in the dead.

The Great Pyramid Tombs

Desmond Stewart

One of the most distinct and famous aspects of ancient Egyptian religion was tomb-building, especially the construction of large-scale stone pyramids to serve as final resting places of pharaohs and other nobles. Popular opinion, shaped by periodic articles, books, and television programs by amateurs and sensationalists, often holds that no one knows how the pyramids were built or that the ancient Egyptians did not have the skill or tools to erect such huge and mathematically precise structures; and therefore, aliens or perhaps some kind of mystical or supernatural forces must have played a part in their construction. This line of thinking is misguided and completely without foundation. Reputable scholars have long had a relatively clear general idea of how the Egyptians built these monuments, even if they are unsure of some of the details. The fact is that what they lacked in the way of modern measuring and lifting devices, the builders amply made up for in their access to nearly unlimited amounts of labor, time, patience, and native ingenuity. The following summary of the development of these tombs and the steps in pyramid construction is by Desmond Stewart, a noted authority on Near Eastern history and culture. He cites the evidence provided by the ancient Greek historians Herodotus (fifth century B.C.) and Diodorus Siculus (first century B.C.) in describing the building of the pyramid tombs, including the largest of all, that of the pharaoh Khufu (or Cheops).

The development of the Egyptian royal tomb from a burial pit to the triumphant Great Pyramid is a logical sequence of responses to funerary needs. Take, for example, the reputed grave of Narmer's successor, King Aha, which has been excavated at Sakkara on the plateau overlooking Memphis. It is little more

Desmond Stewart, *The Pyramids and Sphinx*. New York: Newsweek Book Division, 1971. Copyright © 1971 by Arnoldo Mondadori Editore, S.p.A. Reproduced by permission.

than a shallow pit, divided by five partitions. The king's body was once housed in its middle compartment, and the pit was roofed with wood. On top rose a brick superstructure divided into twenty-seven chambers for storing utensils and food. This oblong superstructure acquired the Arabic name *mastaba* in the nineteenth century when Egyptian villagers working for European archaeologists noticed a resemblance to the oblong mud-brick benches on which they sat gossiping in their village homes. The *mastaba* probably imitated the shape of ordinary dwellings of the archaic period.

In the next two dynasties the *mastaba* part of the tomb—the portion of the structure visible aboveground—had become a mere mass of rubble enclosed by stout retaining walls. At the same time the part of the tomb beneath the ground level had vastly expanded. The body itself was buried in a pit sunk deep into the rock. When the substitution of a statue had first been employed, the king's representation had stood at one end of the superstructure, on ground level. Bitter experience soon showed that statues were as liable to be robbed as corpses. As a protective measure the statue had to be placed in an underground chamber to which only priests had access.

Imhotep and the Step Pyramid

Zoser's Step Pyramid at Sakkara marks one of those developments that afterward seem inevitable but that would have been impossible without an experimenting genius. That [the royal official] Imhotep was such a genius we know, not from Greek legend, which identified him with Aesculapius, the god of medicine, but from what archaeologists have discovered from his still impressive pyramid. Investigation has shown that, at every stage, he was prepared to experiment along new lines. His first innovation was to construct a *mastaba* that was not oblong, but square. His second concerned the material from which it was built. Hitherto brick had been used for all buildings, though stone was used here and there for thresholds, floors, or lintels.

Imhotep decided to dress a core of Sakkara limestone with an outer casing of the superior stone from the quarries on the east bank of the Nile. The *mastaba* was 26 feet in height and its sides were 207 feet long, each side being oriented to one of the cardinal points. A dissatisfied Imhotep then extended his great square by about fourteen feet on all four sides. The extension was two feet lower than the original *mastaba*, so that a two-step structure now existed. This may have given Imhotep his next idea for an improvement. This was to enlarge the base and impose three diminishing squares on it to form a four-step pyramid. This still did not satisfy Imhotep or his royal patron, and the original four-step building was soon concealed inside a far more ambitious design—a great step pyramid of six platforms rising to a flat summit just over two hundred feet above ground level.

No document or inscription survives to explain why the true pyramid form was chosen for the monumental tombs of Egypt's kings, or why that form was finally achieved in the second pyramid built by Snofru, founder of the Fourth Dynasty, at Dahshur. (The first was rhomboid, or bent.) Several reasons have been inferred. Although apparently contradictory, these hypotheses are not mutually exclusive . . . so they probably allowed various insights to prompt their architectural designs.

Many architectural motifs in the buildings surrounding the Step Pyramid bear evidence of Mesopotamian influences. The great ziggurats dominating the Lower Euphrates skyline would have been remembered by those who traveled west to Egypt—much as they were remembered by the Hebrews in their legend of the Tower of Babel. Mesopotamia lacked stone; Egypt did not, and once the possibilities of building with stone were realized by the Egyptians, the construction of a man-made mountain in the relatively flat Egyptian landscape became an envisageable temptation. Nothing, they rightly saw, could be so impressive. A pyramid was also the logical development of Imhotep's design: a true pyramid being nothing more than a . . . step pyramid encased so as to present unbroken sides. To a people whose mathematics were already advanced, the appeal of a pure geometric figure must itself have been strong.

Two religious reasons may also have played their part. The king . . . was associated with the cult of the sun-god, Re, whose shrine, "the fountain of the Sun," was at Heliopolis, now a suburb of Cairo and then a religious center known to the Egyptians and the Bible as On. The pyramid shape resembles the sun's rays as they often flare in Egypt, and an early religious text describes the king as using the sun's rays as ramps to ascend to heaven. There was a further link between the pyramid shape and the Re-worship at On in the *ben-ben*, an early sun symbol composed of a phoenix perching on a pyramidal plinth.

Clues to Construction

If the lack of written evidence forces us to guess why the pyramid shape was chosen, the written evidence as to how the pyramids were constructed is positively misleading. It was written by a man to whom the pyramids were older than the Colosseum is to us. Herodotus, the same Greek who identified Menes as the probable unifier of Egypt, was less fortunate in the information he gleaned at Giza. His informants were dragomans [tour guides] whom he mistook for priests, and as a result his trove combines uncheck-able statistics to the effect that 100,000 men took thirty years to complete the Great Pyramid and its causeway. Picturesque details about the laborers' diet—radishes, onions, and garlic were domi-nant items—are included, as are details that we know to be un-true—such as that the builders used tools made of iron and that machines raised the stones from one level to another.

One story's inherent improbability is only rivaled by its charm:

The wickedness of Cheops reached to such a pitch that, when he had spent all his treasures and wanted more, he sent his daugh-ter to the stews [brothels], with orders to procure him a certain sum—how much I cannot say, for I was not told; she procured it, however, and at the same time, bent on leaving a monument which should perpetuate her own memory, she required each man to make her a present of a stone towards the works which she contemplated. With these stones she built the pyramid which stands midmost of the three that are in front of the Great Pyra-mid, measuring along each side a hundred and fifty feet.

Fortunately the pyramids, including those of lesser importance farther south, embody clues as to how they were built. Patient excavation by modern archaeologists has made the pyramids' construction less mysterious than the origins of the kings who built them.

The pyramid builders had certain limited assets. For one thing they could call on considerable reserves of labor. The figure men-tioned by Herodotus—100,000 men—is not impossible, and the

Greek historian's remark that they were rotated in three-month shifts may be nothing more than a distorted recollection of the probable case that work on the pyramids proceeded in stages during the three summer months when the flooding Nile turned the valley into one huge lake. At that season agricultural work became impossible and the fellahin [agricultural peasants] might well have been glad to work on any project that brought them rations of food, quite apart from the fact that such labor was a sacred task connected with the well-being of Egypt. The flooded Nile also made it possible to ferry to the western escarpment stone brought from the quarries of upriver Aswan as well as limestone from the quarries across the Nile Valley.

The greatest asset of the pyramid builders was an unsurpassed organizing talent. Two Western experts on ancient Egyptian building methods, architect Somers Clarke and engineer R. Engelbach, have flatly stated that the rulers of the Old Kingdom [2686–2181 B.C.] were "the best organizers of human labor the

Egypt's first pyramid—the Step Pyramid at Sakkara—was built as a tomb for the pharaoh Zoser.

world has ever seen." This compliment does not seem excessive when the same experts further inform us that "the only mechanical appliances they knew were the lever, the roller, and the use of vast embankments." The split-second skill of the ancient overseers, a modern Egyptian authority on the pyramids has wryly remarked, seems the one talent that has disappeared.

Selecting the Proper Location

The first task of the royal architects—which they probably shouldered early in each king's reign—was to select a site that met certain basic requirements. It had to be on the western edge of the valley, since the evening ridge was the particular realm of the dead. It had to stand above the level of the highest floods, but not so high as to inhibit the ferrying of stone to within a convenient distance. It needed to be reasonably flat, and large enough to accommodate its suburb of courtiers' tombs. The rock must be solid and flawless in view of the giant burden it would have to bear. The local stone should be adequate for the hidden parts of the core.

The Giza plateau met these requirements perfectly.

The next stage was to peg out a base, which in the case of the Great Pyramid covered an area of just over thirteen acres. A knoll of projecting rock inside this area was incorporated into the bulk of added stone. The sides of the giant square, each roughly 755 feet long, faced the four cardinal points; the future entrance would look directly north to the Pole Star.

The next stage, the leveling of the base, was facilitated by techniques derived from Egyptian agriculture. Mud retaining walls such as those used in the valley fields were built around the pegged-out area and the space so formed filled with water. When the water covered all but the central knoll, a grid of trenches was excavated in the rock until the bottom of each trench was at the same distance from the surface of the water. This done, the mud walls were breached and the water allowed to escape. It was then possible to chip away the intervening rock between the trenches and so secure a level square with a protruding knoll around which the Great Pyramid would rise. This method of using water as a gigantic spirit level was so successful that the southeast corner of the pyramid stands only half an inch higher than the northwest corner. Other dimensions were only slightly less precise, there being a difference of 7.9 inches between the longest side—the south—and the shortest side—the north.

Laying Out the Interior

If these dimensions reveal the calm confidence of men who had already achieved an effective calendar, the pyramid's internal design shows men still experimenting. Analysis of the pyramid has revealed their changes of plan. None of these changes affected the external appearance of the Great Pyramid (which retained the pure pyramidal form first achieved by Snofru, the father of Cheops, in his second pyramid at Dahshur) or altered the entrance site, which remained some fifty-five feet above ground level on the north.

The changes concerned the pyramid's main function: the storage of the royal cadaver. Imhotep had constructed Zoser's burial chamber deep in the solid rock beneath the Step Pyramid, and a similar mortuary plan was first devised for Cheops. An entrance corridor was designed to slant downward for almost 350 feet, first through the pyramid itself, then through the rock on which it stood. Finally a short horizontal passage led to a modest chamber, now choked with the rubble left by nineteenth-century explorers.

Only when the pyramid had advanced by several courses was a second plan made: to construct the chamber in the exact center of the pyramid, but not very high above ground level. It was now too late to plan for a corridor leading straight from the pyramid entrance to the pyramid's heart. Instead, the roof of the descending corridor was pierced and a new ascending corridor (the one in which you bend your back today) was constructed. This culminated, under the second plan, in a horizontal passage leading to the misnamed Queen's Chamber, intended for Cheops. (His queens were in fact buried under the three smaller pyramids that still survive to the east of the Great Pyramid.) This second attempt was next abandoned for a third, more ambitious design—one that involved the construction of the Grand Gallery with its corbeled roof and King's Chamber of granite.

No improvisation such as had modified the corridor system for the second plan was involved in the third. The Gallery and King's Chamber were built from plans as the pyramid nudged skyward, layer by layer. Wooden scaffolding, erected inside the Grand

Gallery, supported great stone plugs that could be lowered immediately after the funeral so as to block forever the ascending corridor. The workmen responsible for closing off the Gallery arranged for their own future: a well-like shaft was bored down to meet the original descending corridor in the rock; having sealed the access route they could then escape, pulling a trapdoor after them.

Transporting the Stones

It was long a puzzle how more than two million stones—the nine granite slabs roofing the King's Chamber average forty-four tons—were raised on the ascending layers. Most historians reached the conclusion that a Greek contemporary of Julius Caesar, Diodorus Siculus, was on the right track when he wrote that the pyramid had been constructed by the use of "mounds," or ramps. His view was theoretically endorsed by Somers Clarke and Engelbach, since they knew that the Old Kingdom Egyptians, who lacked practical knowledge of the wheel, capstan, and pulley, had relied on manpower for most of their haulage. This view found practical confirmation when the unfinished step pyramid of a successor to Zoser was excavated at Sakkara. Ramps made of rubble and builders' waste were found still in place. The remains of one such ramp almost certainly underlie the road by which the modern visitor approaches the Giza plateau.

These ramps were probably of two kinds. Long, broad supply mounds gave an easy incline for the blocks of cut stone, which were edged forward on rollers whose only lubricants were milk or water. Shorter, more sharply pitched ramps probably raised workmen and lighter materials close to the working face. The outer casing, which filled the triangular gap between each layer and the next, was probably laid stage by stage as the work rose higher. When the apex had been reached and the granite capstone placed in position, the ramp would have been removed and the limestone casing smoothed and polished till a seamless sheet reflected the sun by day and the moon by night.

Exploring the Passageways Within the Great Pyramid

I.E.S. Edwards

The so-called Great Pyramid at Giza (near modern-day Cairo) was erected to house the body of the Old Kingdom pharaoh Khufu (whom the Greeks called Cheops). The interior of the structure contains a complex series of corridors and chambers that were not fully explored, mapped, and understood until the twentieth century. Only then did it become clear to archaeologists that the builders originally planned to put Khufu's burial chamber beneath the pyramid. They actually created the chamber, but later changed their minds and carved out a new chamber higher up, inside the body of the structure. This informative description of the pyramid's twisting corridors and the various unused burial chambers is by the late and noted English archaeologist I.E.S. Edwards.

The chambers and corridors of the Great Pyramid, if their arrangement is to be understood, must be considered in conjunction with its structural development. In contrast with the Pyramid of Meidum, the transformations which the Great Pyramid underwent in the course of construction were mainly, if not entirely, internal; its ultimate external shape and dimensions were probably those intended from the beginning.

The Original Burial Chamber

The entrance is in the north face at a height of about 55 feet, measured vertically, above ground-level. It is not situated exactly midway across the face, but at a point about 24 feet east of the centre. From the entrance a corridor, measuring about 3 feet 5 inches in width and 3 feet 11 inches in height, descends at a gradient of 26° 31′ 23′ first through the core of the Pyramid and

I.E.S. Edwards, *The Pyramids of Egypt*. Baltimore: Penguin Books, 1947. Copyright © 1947 by Penguin Books. Reproduced by permission.

then through the rock. At a distance of about 345 feet from the original entrance, the corridor becomes level and continues horizontally for a further 29 feet before terminating in a chamber. On the west side of the level section of the corridor, near the entrance to the chamber, there is a recess, the cutting of which was never completed. The chamber also is unfinished, its trenched floor and rough walls resembling a quarry. A square pit sunk in the floor may represent the first stage in an unfulfilled project for deepening the chamber. . . .

In the south wall of the chamber, opposite the entrance, there is an opening to a blind passage, roughly hewn in the rock and obviously unfinished. The presence of this passage suggests that, if the original plan had been executed, there would have been a second chamber beyond the first and connected with it by a corridor. Such an arrangement would have as a parallel Seneferu's Pyramid at Dahshur, the main difference being that in the latter the second chamber lies directly beneath the apex and the first to the north of it, whereas in the Great Pyramid both chambers would have been situated south of a point perpendicularly [vertically] under the apex.

It is of some interest to compare the half-finished rock-chamber with the brief but graphic description of the subterranean part of the Great Pyramid given to [the Greek historian] Herodotus when he visited Egypt in the middle of the fifth century B.C. Beneath the Pyramid, he was told, were vaults constructed on a kind of island, which was surrounded by water brought from the Nile by a canal. On this island the body of Cheops was said to lie. No trace, however, of either the canal or the island has yet been found, and it is most unlikely that they ever existed. Although the Pyramid had almost certainly been opened and its contents plundered long before the time of Herodotus, it may easily have been closed again. . . . The story which Herodotus relates—the veracity of which he does not claim to have confirmed from his own observations—may well have been embroidered by generations of Pyramid guides extending over the greater part of two centuries.

At the time when the decision was made to alter the original project and to substitute a burial chamber in the body of the Pyramid for the one under construction in the rock, the superstructure had already been built to a height of several feet. A hole was therefore cut in the masonry-roof of the earlier Descending Corridor at a point about 60 feet from the entrance and a new Ascending Corridor was hewn upwards through the core. The mouth of this corridor was filled, after the burial, with a slab of limestone, so that became indistinguishable from the remainder of the roof at the upper end of the Descending Corridor. . . .

The Ascending Corridor, which is approximately 129 feet in length, corresponds in width and height with the Descending Corridor; its gradient of 26° 2′ 30′ also tallies to within a fraction of a degree. At its lower end, immediately above the gap left by the missing limestone slab, are three large plug-blocks made of granite and placed one behind another. . . .

When the Ascending Corridor was being constructed, the builders probably intended the burial-chamber to occupy a position in the centre of the superstructure and at no great height above ground-level. Such a chamber was actually built at the end of a passage leading from the top of the Ascending Corridor. Called by the Arabs the "Queen's Chamber"—a misnomer which it has retained—this chamber lies exactly midway between the north and south sides of the Pyramid. Its measurements are 18 feet 10 inches from east to west and 17 feet 2 inches from north to south. It has a pointed roof, which rises to a height of 20 feet 5 inches. In the east wall there is a niche with corbelled sides; its original depth was only 3 feet 5 inches, but the back has now been cut away by treasure-seekers. Its height is 15 feet 4 inches and the width at the base 5 feet 2 inches. Presumably it was designed to contain a statue of the king, which may, however, never have been placed in position.

There are many indications that work on the Queen's Chamber was abandoned before it had been completed. The floor, for instance, is exceedingly rough; if the chamber had been finished it would probably have been paved with finer stone. Again, in the north and south walls there are small rectangular apertures from which shafts run horizontally for a distance of about 6 feet 6 inches and then turn upwards at an angle of approximately 30°. These apertures were not cut at the time when the chamber was built—an ommission which can only be explained on the hypothesis that the chamber was never finished. . . .

The Grand Gallery

The abandonment of the Queen's Chamber led to the construction of two of the most celebrated architectural works which have survived from the Old Kingdom, namely the Grand Gallery and the King's Chamber. The Grand Gallery was built as a continuation of the Ascending Corridor. It is 153 feet in length and 28 feet in height. Its walls of polished limestone rise vertically to a height of 7 feet 6 inches; above that level each of the seven courses projects inwards about 3 inches beyond the course on which it rests, thus forming a corbel vault of unparalleled dimensions. The space between the uppermost course on each side, measuring 3 feet 5 inches in width, is spanned by roofing slabs, every one of which is laid at a slightly steeper angle than the gradient of the gallery. [The great archaeologist] Sir Flinders Petrie, commenting on this method of laying the slabs, says that it was done "in order that the lower edge of each stone should hitch like a pawl into a ratchet cut in the top of the walls; hence no stone can press on the one below it, so as to cause a cumula-

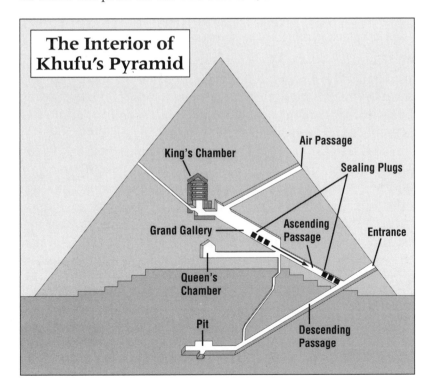

The Interior of Khufu's Pyramid

King's Chamber

Air Passage

Sealing Plugs

Grand Gallery

Ascending Passage

Entrance

Queen's Chamber

Pit

Descending Passage

tive pressure all down the roof; and each stone is separately up-
held by the side-walls across which it lies." At the foot of each
wall a flat-topped ramp, 2 feet in height and 1 foot 8 inches in
width, extends along the whole length of the gallery. A passage
measuring, like the roof, 3 feet 5 inches in width runs between
the two ramps. At the lower end of this passage there is now a
gap, caused by the removal of the stones which formerly linked
the floor of the passage with that of the Ascending Corridor and
also covered the mouth of the horizontal passage leading to the
Queen's Chamber. In the gap, the lowest stone in the western
ramp has been removed, revealing a shaft which descends, partly
perpendicularly and partly obliquely, first through the core of the
Pyramid and then through the rock, until it emerges in the west
wall of the Descending Corridor. Its apparent purpose and the
significance of some other peculiar features in the Grand Gallery
will be considered after the King's Chamber has been described.

The King's Chamber

A high step at the upper end of the Grand Gallery gives access to
a low and narrow passage leading to the King's Chamber. About
a third of the distance along its length, the passage is heightened
and enlarged into a kind of antechamber, the south, east and
west walls of which are composed of red granite. Four wide slots
have been cut in both the east and west walls of the antechamber, three extending to the floor and one—the northernmost—
stopping at the same level as the roof of the passage. . . .

The King's Chamber, built entirely of granite, measures 34 feet
4 inches from east to west, 17 feet 2 inches from north to south,
and 19 feet 1 inch in height. In the north and south walls, at a
height of about 3 feet above the floor, are the rectangular apertures of shafts which differ from those of the Queen's Chamber
only in penetrating the core of the Pyramid to the outer surface,
the northern at an angle of 31° and the southern at an angle of
45°. The object of these shafts is not known with certainty; they
may have been designed for the ventilation of the chamber or for
some religious purpose which is still open to conjecture. Near the
west wall stands a lidless rectangular granite sarcophagus which
once contained the king's body, probably enclosed within an inner coffin of wood. In appearance it is rough, many of the

scratches made by the saw when cutting it being still clearly visible. Sir Flinders Petrie discovered that the width of the sarcophagus was about an inch greater than the width of the Ascending Corridor at its mouth; he therefore concluded that it must have been placed in position while the chamber was being built.

The roof of the King's Chamber has no exact architectural parallel. Above its flat ceiling, which is composed of nine slabs weighing in aggregate about 400 tons, there are five separate compartments, the ceilings of the first four being flat and the fifth having a pointed roof. The purpose of this construction, it appears, was to eliminate any risk of the ceiling of the chamber collapsing under the weight of the superincumbent masonry [stones lying directly above]. Whether such extreme precautions were required by the character of the building may be debatable; they have, however, been justified by subsequent events. Every one of the nine slabs of granite which form the ceiling of the chamber and many of those in the relieving compartments have been cracked—presumably by an earthquake—but none has yet collapsed.

Access to the lowest of the relieving compartments is gained by a passage leading from a hole at the top of the east wall of the Grand Gallery. When or by whom this passage was cut is unknown; the first European to mention it was a traveller named Davison who visited the Pyramid in 1765. The four upper compartments were not discovered until 1837–38, when Colonel Howard Vyse and J.S. Perring forced a way to them by hollowing out a shaft from below. Some of the walls in these upper compartments are composed of limestone; since they were not intended to be seen their surfaces were not dressed and, in consequence, many of the blocks still retain the red ochre marking painted on them at the quarry.

Lost City of the Pyramid Workers

Jack McClintock

A number of archaeologists had long suspected that extensive settlements had been built on the Giza plateau during the Old Kingdom to house the workers who erected the great pyramids and other royal tombs. But for a long time the search for such villages took a backseat to excavations of the tombs themselves. Then, beginning in the late 1990s, American archaeologist Mark Lehner and Egyptian archaeologist Zahi Hawass led a team that has so far found thousands of artifacts belonging to houses, bakeries, tool shops, and other facilities set up on the plateau during pyramid construction. This informative overview of how these excavations came about and what they have uncovered so far is by science writer Jack McClintock.

The hat is in the hole. Crouched on one knee under the searing sun a few hundred yards south of the Sphinx . . . Mark Lehner sweeps dust with a paintbrush from the remains of an ancient wall. . . . Since he unearthed this wall just a week ago, he has hardly stopped thinking about it. Could it be the royal palace he's been seeking—home of those who ruled the workers who built the pyramids?

For nearly 30 years, Lehner, a respected authority on ancient Egypt's Sphinx and pyramids, has labored to answer a perplexing question: Where did the more than 20,000 people who built these mysterious monuments live? He is convinced the people lived right here on the Giza plateau, in a lost city that is among the world's oldest, dating from roughly 2500 B.C. So far, he's found plenty of evidence of their work—but thousands of houses, if they exist, still lie invisible beneath the sand.

"We're finding the everyday structures that supported the pyramid-building," says Lehner. . . ."We know from tomb scenes

Jack McClintock, "Lost City," *Discover*, October 2001. Copyright © 2001 by Jack McClintock. Reproduced by permission.

that the people who lived here baked bread, and now we've found the real thing—real bakeries. We've found real streets, real galleries, a great production complex organized in long streets and corridors. . . . It's the largest exposure of an Old-Kingdom [2575–2130 B.C.] settlement, where Egyptians actually carried out work, as opposed to just building tombs and monuments." He pauses. "But why did we find enough bones to have fed 6,000 people a day if they ate meat daily—which they probably didn't—but no houses? Where were all the people? It's very strange, and very cool that we don't know—because that means we're onto something."

Just this week, after decades of digging and measuring, Lehner thinks he may have found a royal residence, home of the ruler whom the laborers served. But in an e-mail dispatch sent home to financial supporters, he doesn't permit himself to use the word *palace*. So far it's just a "double-walled, buttressed building." He has exposed only a corner of it. He knows that Egyptian royal residences tended to be oriented cleanly from north to south, as this building is, while the rest of the complex is skewed significantly clockwise. If this structure does turn out to be a palace, it will clinch Lehner's notion that there was a workers' city at Giza—no palace could exist without people living nearby to sustain it. And this building is big. Very big. Lehner's hat-shaded face shows surprise, hope, and excitement. "I'm very intrigued by this," he says carefully. "It's possibly fairly significant. It's very suggestive. I can't say, but it looks like a big deal.". . .

Lehner's First Trips to Giza

In 1979 the American Research Center in Egypt agreed to sponsor his first major project: mapping the Sphinx. "Although it's the most prominent of Middle Eastern monuments, it had never been carefully studied until Mark went at it," says Peter Lacovara, curator of ancient art at the Michael C. Carlos Museum at Emory University in Atlanta. Lehner spent five years clambering across the 66-foot colossus, measuring every stone with a folding rule and a tape measure, dropping his plumb bob from every conceivable height. He carefully triangulated nearly 100 separate points on the face alone. "I was a good mapper, a good artistic hand," he says, "and I really fell in love with it." He produced a detailed scale drawing six feet long, and as he unrolls it today on the dining room floor of the villa he rents in Giza, he smiles. "I tell people, 'Pick a block, check it out, keep me honest.'" He says no one has yet found an error. When the Sphinx was restored, starting in the late 1980s, Lehner's map was invaluable.

Over the years Lehner came to know the Giza plateau intimately. He learned its geology, its history, its archaeology, and used them all to understand how the plateau had evolved. Originally it formed as a shell embankment beneath the sea. When the waters receded 50 million years ago, during the Eocene Epoch, the plateau became dry land. Today it consists of a limestone plate called the Mokattam Formation: a high, fossil-packed embankment to the northwest, on which the pyramids were built, and a slope of alternating layers of hard and soft limestone to the southeast, where the Sphinx lies.

On the advice of a friend, Lehner began approaching the plateau from the south, rather than from the north and east as

Bakeries and Fish Houses

In this excerpt from an article in Archaeology, *Zahi Hawass and Mark Lehner provide details about the workers' bakeries and other food processing facilities they excavated on the Giza plateau in the late 1990s.*

Just before our 1991 season a backhoe digging sand for use in a construction project dug through ancient walls, floors, and thousands of potsherds about 820 feet northeast of the pedestal building. In cleaning out the trench we discovered a series of stone-rubble wall foundations. The walls had formed about a dozen rooms attached to the larger mud-brick sides of a massive building. The backhoe had dug into the southeast corner of the building, just missing two complete ceramic vats situated in two adjacent, parallel rooms. Excavation of these rooms, under the supervision of Michael Chazan of Harvard University, made it clear that they were bakeries like those shown in Old Kingdom tomb scenes and models.

Each bakery was about 17 feet long and eight feet wide. Inside each room lay a pile of broken bread pots discarded after the last batch of bread was removed 4,600 years ago. Though Egyptian written records attest at least 14 types of bread, we found only small and large bell-shaped pots and flat trays. Along the east wall were two lines of holes in a shallow trench, resembling an egg carton. The holes had held dough-filled pots while hot coals and ash in the trench baked most tourists do. He spent many afternoons on top of a windy knoll, contemplating the layered, pitted landscape geologists had described. Eventually he had read so much, talked to so many scholars, and lain awake so many nights thinking how the monuments might have been built that a picture began forming in his head—"my epiphany [sudden realization or awakening] in the desert," he calls it. In his mind, he saw kilt-clad workers toiling in the quarries, cutting through the softer layers of limestone blocks with copper chisels and stone pickaxes. He saw granite-laden boats sailing down the Nile from Aswan and into a canal-fed harbor. He imagined other boats bringing finer limestone from Tura, just across the Nile, to encase the pyramids in gleaming white. Lehner came to understand how thousands of years ago someone else, Khufu's architect, might have envisioned this place: where to place the quarries, the canals, the workshops—the city.

Lehner knew that he would need further academic training

the bread. A hearth in the southeastern corner would have been used to heat pots before they were inverted as lids on dough-filled containers in the trench. Low walls of stone and mud around the rooms were used as counter space to store pots and finished loaves.

The bakeries were attached to the back of a much larger mud-brick building enclosed by a five-foot-thick wall. In 1991 we cleared part of this building's floor. Here we found low partition walls and two sets of low benches, formed of black alluvial mud and covered with *tafla*, separated by troughs. In one place we found a group of complete jar stands and lids (but no jars) on the benches. In early 1995, with John Nolan of the University of Chicago, we explored the building further, exposing more sets of long parallel troughs and benches, which ran across the floor of a broad court and continued north and west beyond our excavation. Embedded in the floor were fibrous bits and pieces, the remains of fish gills and fins. . . .

We believe this was a food processing installation. We found an assortment of flint blades and flakes alongside the benches. These may have been used for cleaning fish that were then dried and perhaps smoked and salted. One of the benches had been built around two limestone bases for wooden columns. Tomb scenes show meat being dried on lines tied between small columns.

Zahi Hawass and Mark Lehner, "Builders of the Pyramids," *Archaeology,* January/February 1997, p. 34.

and credentials to continue his search, so he returned to the United States in 1985 to study for a Ph.D. in archaeology at Yale. In 1990 he took a job teaching Egyptian archaeology at the University of Chicago, but Giza fever was in his blood. . . .

While he was teaching, his friend, archaeologist Zahi Hawass, now Director of the Pyramids, began digging at Giza, less than a half mile south of the pyramids. Over time, Hawass has discovered the graves of 600 skilled tomb builders and 82 larger tombs of overseers and artisans. Skeletal remains inside told of men who had worked hard and died in their thirties. Some had healed fractures, others had endured successful amputations, suggesting sophisticated medical treatment. Hawass and Lehner say this quality of care argues that they weren't slaves. "Why do we think first of slavery and coercion?" Lehner says rhetorically. "I think we think slaves because of our inherited biblical and classical traditions. It is hard for us—used to such individual liberty and wage labor—to conceive of life in a more traditional society. We cannot assume they reacted, acted, thought, and felt the way we do about obligations to the greater community." More likely, he says . . . they were peasant laborers who rotated into and out of work parties. Graffiti carved by workers in places that were never meant to be seen show that they proudly named themselves "Friends of Khufu" and "Drunkards of Menkaure." They had built the mighty leaders' monuments—and miniature versions for themselves.

A Total Information Package

Lehner grew increasingly restless in Chicago as Hawass's work revealed a story much like the one he'd written in his imagination years earlier. Knowing that workers had been buried next to the monuments they'd built, he grew more certain that they must also have lived nearby. Although Lehner had spent some time in Giza each year, digging a few 16½-foot-square "windows in the sand," as he calls them, it was not enough. In 1995 he packed his trowel, put on his green felt hat, and headed for Egypt.

Back in Giza, Lehner threw himself into digging in the southeast corner of the plateau, just south of the Sphinx and downhill from the workers' cemetery. The site was one of the last unexcavated areas around the base of the plateau, a spot where local residents tossed trash and stable litter. Lehner's team collected, recorded, and studied everything: plant remains, animal bones, ceramics, stones, charcoal, and pressed-mud sealings, labels of quick-drying mud stamped with hieroglyphics. "They're a real asset because generally there aren't many texts here, and they provide names of kings, officials, institutions," he says. Sealings collected here suggest that the site dates as far back as Khufu, builder of the first pyramid. Unlike earlier explorers, who just plunged into the sand with shovels or even tried to blow holes in the pyramids with dynamite, Lehner is doing this dig by the book, preserving every tiny piece of evidence. "We're getting a total information package on the plateau—environment, climate, migratory paths of birds," he says. "We've had specialists in hearths, in animal bone, in ceramics, in lithics. We've salvaged 300,000 fragments of charcoal, 18,000 bits of labeled stone chips, 650 paleobotanical samples, 100,000 pottery shards." A thrilling moment for Lehner was finding where the bread was made that fed the multitudes: "We found the bakeries, the tail of the tiger—this huge archaeological animal." After he identified the bakeries—small rooms where huge loaves were baked in heavy, bell-shaped clay pots—"we started chasing the walls," Lehner says.

In another square, Lehner found a copper works with a small clay furnace, then a few small chambers similar to workers' houses found at other sites in Egypt. He found the hypostyle hall—so called because of its column-supported roof—lined with low benches separated by troughs. Everywhere they dug, workers found the butchered bones of cattle, sheep, and goats. In 1998, Lehner cleared a 66-foot-square area and found a series of galleries: long, narrow, corridorlike enclosures that were complex structures with plastered walls. By this point Lehner's vision had grown. "It's been a hypothesis of mine that all this is connected to a palace," he says. "You don't just have production facilities by themselves. They're always connected to a lord."

Despite all the discoveries, Lehner grew frustrated. His windows in the sand provided only tantalizing glimpses. He knew there was more to his quest than mud huts and palaces. Old-Kingdom Egypt had been poised at a crucial cultural threshold, "moving from an informal, small-scale village society to a complex bureaucratic state." Anything he could learn about this transformation would shed light on the evolution of one of the world's earliest nation-states. . . .

Where Are the Houses?

Excavation began in the fall of 1999. By last summer [2001], using a diesel-powered front loader, hand trowels, and paintbrushes, Lehner's team had cleared and staked a hectare, the equivalent of 400 of his 16½-foot-squares. As the team continued to dig, Lehner's little snapshots in the sand widened into a panorama—more than a dozen bakeries, a pigment-grinding shop, the copper works, and lots of bones. He found more galleries and realized there were workrooms tucked in the back of living spaces. He found an avenue and three main streets, one of them among the oldest paved roads in the world. At either end, he uncovered two larger structures, dubbed the Manor House and the Gatehouse, checkpoints from which anyone entering or leaving the workrooms could have been seen. It was a two-year marathon, Lehner says.

Sometimes, when the others are at lunch, Lehner can be seen pacing alone in the sun, his arms folded across his chest and his head down, just thinking. He has begun to visualize the stirrings of a nation-state. If the site reveals how the Egyptians built the pyramids, Lehner believes, it also tells a little about how the pyramids built Egypt. Only a grand project like this one could have united a widely scattered agrarian people and cemented them into a larger society.

But where are the houses? More than likely, Lehner says, they lie buried beneath the soccer field on the edge of his authorized site or beneath a densely populated town to the east. After all, he says, this dig has uncovered only a corner of the lost city. Like the city, his enigmatic, double-walled buttressed building—a palace?—appears to reach well beyond the site's boundaries. How far does it go? What, exactly, is it? What will it tell us about Egyptian history? Lehner is uncertain. But, he says, smiling and removing his hat . . . "I came here in search of a lost civilization, and I did find a civilization, a major part of which is lost. Truly, there is a lost city of the pyramids."

Opening King Tut's Tomb

Steven Snape

Most of the tombs of the Egyptian pharaohs were looted by robbers within a few years, or a few centuries at most, after they were sealed. One, however, belonging to the boy-king Tutankhamen (who ruled from 1336 to 1327 B.C.), better known as "King Tut," survived the ages almost intact. (Ancient thieves did manage to break in; but for reasons unknown they abandoned their operation before stealing much.) In 1922, an English archaeologist located the tomb in the Valley of the Kings, a vast royal necropolis (burial area) on the Nile's west bank a few miles from modern Luxor. (In all, sixty-two pharaohs were interred in the valley.) This synopsis of how Howard Carter found the tomb and the exciting moment when he first laid eyes on its long-hidden contents is by University of Liverpool scholar Steven Snape.

For Howard Carter the discovery of the tomb of Tutankhamen was the culmination of a thirty-year obsession with ancient Egypt; his life was never to be the same again.

The son of an impoverished Norfolk animal painter, Carter (1874–1939) was an outstanding excavator and draughtsman, but a solitary, irascible [temperamental] man of little formal education. Dependent for much of his career on aristocratic patrons, he began work as an artist at the age of seventeen copying paintings on the walls of the rock-cut tombs at Beni Hassan for the pioneer British Egyptologist Francis Llewellyn Griffith. A year later he had his first taste of excavation under the direction of [noted archaeologist] Flinders Petrie, appropriately enough at el-Amarna, the short-lived capital founded in upper Egypt by Tutankamen's probable father, the heretic pharaoh Akhenaten (d. 1337 B.C.).

In 1899 Carter was made Inspector-General of Monuments of

Steven Snape, "Tutankhamen and the Glint of Gold," *The Cambridge Illustrated History of Archaeology*, edited by Paul G. Bahn. New York: Cambridge University Press, 1996.

Upper Egypt, an important new post in the Egyptian Antiquities Service. A similar appointment in Lower Egypt followed, but he was not to retain this post for long: in 1905 a brawl at the burial ground of Saqqara near Memphis between drunken French tourists and Antiquities Service guards ended with Carter ejecting the tourists by force. Affronted, they demanded an apology through the French consul in Cairo; Carter, with characteristic obstinacy, refused to provide one and resigned.

Into the Valley of the Kings

An experienced Egyptologist with negligible employment prospects, Carter was now lucky enough to meet George Herbert, fifth earl of Carnarvon (1866–1923), a languid and immensely rich English aristocrat whose early love of racehorses and fast cars had given way in middle age to an equal passion for archaeology. Carnarvon had dug in a small way at Thebes in 1907, but soon realised that he needed a professional archaeologist like Carter to provide his work with credibility and technical direction. For five years (1907–11) Carter and Carnarvon together excavated in the private cemeteries on the west bank of the Nile at Thebes, extending their work to the Nile delta in 1912–13.

The delta excavations proved disappointing, so the acquisition in 1914 of one of the most sought-after excavating concessions in Egypt, that of the Valley of the Kings, was doubly welcome. Carter began work in the valley in 1915–16 by clearing the known tombs of [the pharaohs] Amenhotep III and Hatchepsut, but by 1917 his activities were focused on the search for just one tomb, that of Tutankhamen.

Since no burial place was known, Carter concluded that the pharaoh's hidden and probably unrobbed tomb must exist somewhere nearby. Five barren years later anyone less cussedly determined and less well funded would have given up the search, but Carter persuaded Carnarvon to continue the concession for just one more season, offering to pay for the work himself if need be. He wanted to investigate the only remaining undug area on the floor of the valley, a small triangle in front of the tomb of Ramesses VI, left until then so as not to disrupt tourist access to the tomb.

Wonderful Things

The excavation season began on 1 November 1922. Three days later, beneath ancient workmens' huts, Carter found the first rock-cut step leading down to Tutankhamen's tomb; the following day he located the plastered blocking to the entrance and wired Carnarvon in England to announce his discovery—a sensation soon to grab headlines the world over. Finally, on 26 November, Carter, accompanied now by Carnarvon, broke into the tomb and gazed into the antechamber—one of the great moments in the history of archaeology.

> At first I could see nothing, the hot air escaping from the chamber causing the candle to flicker, but presently, as my eyes grew accustomed to the light, details of the room emerged slowly from

---

The Boy-King's Burial Objects

More than two thousand objects were found in Tutankhamen's tomb, a few of which are described here by noted scholar Lionel Casson.

A pharaoh who was ready for the afterlife was buried amid symbols of his might. Tutankhamen's tomb was full of such objects—many, such as his throne, simply taken from the palace. Most of the furnishings attest to the Pharaoh's exalted power. Although the young Tutankhamen probably never saw a battlefield, one small medallion honors his official (if not actual) prowess as a soldier. Amid the signs of impersonal pomp there are also occasional domestic touches—for example the picture on his throne of [his wife], young Queen Ankhesnamum, making a wifely adjustment of the King's costume. When Tutankhamen's mummy was sealed away in its tomb, the priests saw to it that the dead King, reawakened, would find about him all the accustomed comforts and accoutrements of palace life. They supplied the tomb with over 100 baskets of fruit to feed him, feathered fans to cool him, statues of servants to wait on him. There were an exquisite centerpiece; a beautiful vase to hold oils; two finely wrought ceremonial knives, probably intended for a royal military expedition. As added equipment for such an expedition, the priests buried two chariots and even a folding camp bed.

Besides such traditional objects of royal pleasure, Tutankhamen's tomb contained some special mementos of the young King's childhood. Included among these were a toy-box and a painting set.

Lionel Casson, *Ancient Egypt*. New York: Time-Life, 1965, pp. 171–72.

the mist, strange animals, statues, and gold—everywhere the glint of gold. For the moment—an eternity it must have seemed to the others standing by—I was struck dumb with amazement, and when Lord Carnarvon, unable to stand the suspense any longer, inquired anxiously 'Can you see anything?', it was all I could do to get out the words 'Yes, wonderful things'.

More wonderful things were to follow for the antechamber was just one of four principal rooms heaped, as Carnarvon wrote, with 'beds, boxes and every conceivable thing'. The burial chamber itself proved to contain the mummy of the pharaoh encased in three coffins, the innermost of solid gold, as well as a massive quartzite sarcophagus and three shrines of gilded wood, one inside another.

Once the initial sensation had died down, Carter was left with the problem of how to deal with so stupendous a find. Money . . . came from Carnarvon and an exclusive, though politically maladroit [inept], newspaper deal with *The Times* of London. Carter was also able to put together a formidable team of specialists from museums around the world, notably the photographer Harry Burton from the Metropolitan Museum in New York, and from Cairo the chemist and conservator Alfred Lucas, who set up a field laboratory in the empty tomb of Seti II nearby. Slowly the work of recording, conserving, and removing to Cairo the thousands of objects from the tomb got under way. It was a task that occupied Carter and his team for the next ten years.

Within weeks of disturbing the tomb, on 5 April 1923, Lord Carnarvon died in Cairo of pneumonia following a septic mosquito bite. The legend of 'the curse of Tutankhamen' was born. Carter himself died peacefully some sixteen years later in his elegant London apartment close to Hyde Park, his retirement in England lonely and dogged by illness but his status in the archaeological pantheon secure for all time.

Chronology

B.C.

ca. 5500–3100
Years of Egypt's Predynastic Period, in which two or more kingdoms coexist and likely compete in the Nile Valley.

ca. 3150–3100
A powerful ruler named Menes (or Narmer) unites the kingdoms of Upper and Lower Egypt, creating the world's first true nation-state.

ca. 2700–2180
Years of the Old Kingdom, during which most of Egypt's pyramids are built, including the largest ones, at Giza, near modern Cairo.

2598–2566
Reign of the pharaoh Khufu (whom the Greeks called Cheops), who erects the largest of all the pyramids for his tomb.

2050–1650
Years of the Middle Kingdom, in which the Egyptians begin expanding their territory by conquest and their wealth through trade.

1650–1550
Years in which Egypt is occupied by the Hyksos, a warlike Near Eastern people who take over northern Egypt.

1550–1070
Years of the New Kingdom, in which a series of vigorous pharaohs create an Egyptian empire.

1479–1425
Reign of Thutmose III, greatest of Egypt's conqueror-kings, who rules the empire at its largest extent.

1352–1336

Reign of Amenhotep IV, who changes his name to Akhenaten in the process of launching a religious revolution in which he favors the face of the sun (the Aten) over the traditional Egyptian gods.

1336–1327

Reign of the young and fairly obscure pharaoh Tutankhamen, popularly known today as "King Tut."

1279–1213

Reign of Rameses II, who fights the Hittites (who hail from what is now Turkey) in a great battle (the first in recorded history about which details are known) at Kadesh, in Syria.

1184–1153

Reign of Rameses III, who defeats the Sea Peoples (invaders from the north) near the Nile Delta.

1069–747

Years of the Third Intermediate Period, in which the strong nation established during the New Kingdom becomes disunited and undergoes decline.

747–332

Years of the Late Period, during much of which Egypt comes under the rule of foreigners, including Assyrians, Persians, and Greeks. In 332 B.C., Greek conqueror Alexander the Great enters Egypt, liberating it from the Persians, but at the same time introducing Greek culture and political dominance.

331

Alexander establishes Alexandria in the eastern Nile Delta. The city quickly becomes one of the greatest and most prosperous in the Mediterranean world, eventually second only to Rome.

323

Death of Alexander. Soon afterward, one of his generals, Ptolemy, makes himself pharaoh of Egypt, beginning a new royal line, the Ptolemaic.

31

Cleopatra VII, last of the Ptolemies, and the last independent ruler of Egypt, is defeated by the Romans at Actium, in Greece. The following year, she commits suicide and Rome makes Egypt a province in its own empire.

A.D.

639–642

Arab armies seize control of Egypt from the Byzantine Empire, which had inherited the area when the western Roman Empire disintegrated in the prior century. The Arabs introduce the Arabic language and the religion of Islam.

1798

French conqueror Napoléon invades Egypt, bringing along over a hundred scholars to study the country's ancient monuments.

1799

Discovery of the Rosetta Stone, which proves to be the key to deciphering hieroglyphics, the picture language used by the ancient Egyptians.

1922

English archaeologist Howard Carter enters King Tut's tomb, which proves to be filled with golden artifacts, a find that creates a worldwide sensation.

1990s

Archaeologists begin unearthing the remains of the settlements that housed the workers who erected the great pyramids at Giza.

For Further Research

Ancient Sources in Translation

J.H. Breasted, ed. and trans., *Ancient Records of Egypt*. 5 vols. New York: Russell and Russell, 1962.

———, trans., *The Edwin Smith Surgical Papyrus*. Chicago: University of Chicago Press, 1930.

C.D.N. Costa, trans. and ed., *Seneca: Dialogues and Letters*. New York: Penguin Books, 1997.

Herodotus, *Histories*, trans. Aubrey de Sélincourt. New York: Penguin Books, 1972.

Miriam Lichtheim, ed., *Ancient Egyptian Literature: A Book of Readings*. 2 vols. Berkeley: University of California Press, 1975–1976.

Josephine Mayer and Tom Prideaux, eds., *Never to Die: The Egyptians in Their Own Words*. New York: Viking, 1938.

James B. Pritchard, ed., *Ancient Near Eastern Texts Relating to the Old Testament*. Princeton: Princeton University Press, 1969.

W.K. Simpson, ed., *The Literature of Ancient Egypt: An Anthology of Stories, Instructions, and Poetry*. New Haven: Yale University Press, 1973.

Modern Sources

Paul G. Bahn, ed., *The Cambridge Illustrated History of Archaeology*. New York: Cambridge University Press, 1996.

Bob Brier, *Egyptian Mummies: Unraveling the Secrets of an Ancient Art*. New York: William Morrow, 1994.

Lionel Casson, *Ancient Egypt*. New York: Time-Life, 1965.

———, *Daily Life in Ancient Egypt*. New York: American Heritage, 1975.

Sergio Donadoni, ed., *The Egyptians*. Trans. Robert Bianchi et al. Chicago: University of Chicago Press, 1990.

I.E.S. Edwards, *The Pyramids of Egypt*. Harmondsworth, England: Penguin Books, 1947.

Adolf Erman, *Life in Ancient Egypt*. Trans. H.M. Tirard. New York: Dover, 1971.

Ahmed Fakhry, *The Pyramids*. Chicago: University of Chicago Press, 1961.

Charles Freeman, *Egypt, Greece, and Rome: Civilizations of the Ancient Mediterranean*. New York: Oxford University Press, 1996.

Nicolas Grimal, *A History of Ancient Egypt*. Trans. Ian Shaw. Oxford, England: Blackwell, 1992.

Zahi Hawass and Mark Lehner, "Builders of the Pyramids," *Archaeology*, January/February 1997.

Jill Kamil, *The Ancient Egyptians: Life in the Old Kingdom*. Cairo: American University in Cairo Press, 1996.

Jack McClintock, "Lost City," *Discover*, October 2001.

Barbara Mertz, *Red Land, Black Land: Daily Life in Ancient Egypt*. New York: Dodd, Mead, 1978.

Lynn Meskell, *Private Life in New Kingdom Egypt*. Princeton: Princeton University Press, 2002.

Don Nardo, *Egyptian Mythology*. Berkeley Heights, NJ: Enslow Publishers, 2000.

James F. Romano, *Daily Life of the Ancient Egyptians*. Pittsburgh: Carnegie Museum of Natural History, 1990.

H.W.F. Saggs, *Civilization Before Greece and Rome*. New Haven: Yale University Press, 1989.

Byron E. Shafer, ed., *Religion in Ancient Egypt*. Ithaca: Cornell University Press, 1991.

Ian Shaw, ed., *The Oxford History of Ancient Egypt*. Oxford, England: Oxford University Press, 2000.

Ian Shaw and Paul Nicholson, *The Dictionary of Ancient Egypt*. New York: Harry N. Abrams, 1995.

David P. Silverman, ed., *Ancient Egypt*. New York: Oxford University Press, 1997.

Chester G. Starr, *A History of the Ancient World*. New York: Oxford University Press, 1991.

Miriam Stead, *Egyptian Life*. London: British Museum, 1986.

Desmond Stewart, *The Pyramids and the Sphinx*. New York: Newsweek Book Division, 1971.

Index

About the Editor

A historian and award-winning writer, Don Nardo has written or edited numerous books about the ancient world. Among these are *Life in Ancient Athens, Greek and Roman Sport, Egyptian Mythology,* and the *Greenhaven Encyclopedia of Ancient Rome.* He lives with his wife, Christine, in Massachusetts.

DATE DUE
